# make your child brilliant

## Uncovering your child's hidden gifts

Bernadette Tynan

# make your child brilliant

Uncovering your child's hidden gifts

Quadrille

For ★ Aaliyah ★ Aisha ★ Connor ★ Molly ★ Nicholas ★ Sophie and all the children in the world. You are brilliant.

First published in 2008 by Quadrille Publishing Limited
Alhambra House
27–31 Charing Cross Road
London WC2H 0LS

This edition produced for The Book People, Hall Wood Avenue, Haydock, St Helens, WA11 9UL

Electric Sky Productions
1 Clifton Mews
Clifton Hill
Brighton
BN1 3HR
www.electricsky.com

**Series Producer:** Sophie Key
**Executive Producer:** Benita Matofska



**Editorial Director:** Jane O'Shea
**Art Director:** Helen Lewis
**Editor:** Emma Callery
**Designer:** Katherine Case
**Illustrations:** All by Katherine Case except the pig on page 53, which is by Bridget Bodoano
**Production:** Vincent Smith and Ruth Deary



Cataloguing-in-Publication Data: a catalogue record for this book is available from the British Library.

ISBN 978 184400 821 6

Printed in China

# Introduction

Massive changes in scientific discoveries about children's brain development have influenced education and learning in recent years. For the first time, this book is designed to make transparent for parents everywhere the implications of these discoveries. For this generation of children, it means being able to discover and develop their individual gifts and talents on a scale unprecedented in previous generations.

Changes in how children think and learn are already afoot in schools worldwide. Take a peek at your child's homework and you have probably spotted already that 'they do things differently' at school now. So different, in fact, that parents often come to me feeling uncertain and confused about how to support and advise their children for the best in today's schools.

I have worked with different families around the world to help their children succeed. Increasingly parents are concerned and want information about a widening area of topics:

★ Are tests a good or a bad thing for my child's brain development?

★ Is ability inherited or can children be good at things that aren't 'in the genes'?

★ Can state-funded schools do just as well as fee-paying schools for children?

★ What are the things I should be looking for when I am thinking about schools for my child?

★ Is it true that the brain never stops growing or is it never too late to change things as children grow older?

★ Is it true that there are different kinds of learning styles, and, if so, how can that benefit my child?

★ Is fun learning really better learning?

★ What if my child is good at something that isn't tested at school, how do I identify that? How would I know?

★ Can the way children learn affect how well they do in the long term?

★ Is there a better way for my child to revise and pass exams?

★ What is accelerated learning – is that better brain learning?

The questions are many and important and that is why I've written this book. It is designed to answer them all and more. Inside its pages is the knowledge that puts to an end ever having to feel in the dark or uncertain about what may or may not be best to ensure a brighter future for your child. Whether your child is just starting school or is right in the middle of the school journey, step by step you will learn how to make widely informed choices about your child's future and move forward confidently.

Each chapter lifts the lid on key concepts in brain development, learning, education, tests and how to identify children's individual gifts. Every child is different. Each child's gifts come in individual packages, and not everything can be captured on standard pen and paper tests. In fact, some children's abilities can be missed completely by standard tests. So, rather than pigeonhole children's abilities, which can leave little room for growth and opportunities, I like to talk about them having clusters of gifts and talents.

## IDENTIFYING AND NURTURING ABILITIES

Much of my success with parents has come from showing them how to identify and cultivate a wide range of abilities in their children. This has enabled parents to provide their children with more choices as they grow and develop. More choice means giving both you and your child more knowledge so that you can make more widely informed decisions.

The steps in this book are designed to enable you to become an expert in your own right in order to discover and develop your child's natural gifts. As you progress through the chapters, both you and your child will discover and learn about facts and techniques that can be used and referred back to whenever you feel the need.

Step by step, I show you how to map out a route to success that sees both you and your child benefit from the knowledge you have gained. Every child has dreams and ambitions that are special to them. Through practical planning and following the route mapped out for you in this book, your child's dreams can start to become realistic and attainable goals. Together, you and your child will learn how to:

★ Identify individual strengths and gifts.

★ Set goals and achieve them.

★ Troubleshoot any problems at school and overcome obstacles.

★ Make learning more effective, personalized and fun.

★ Celebrate success together.

When combined with knowledge about how the brain actually works and in what ways you learn best, these techniques help children to become more confident and self-directed learners. They become less dependent upon others for help and more able, therefore, to get the best out of their school years.

When children have a clear route to success like this, where they have shared in planning and deciding the route with their parents, they are more likely to know where they are going. Even better, they know how they are going to get there. They are well on their way to realizing their own individual gifts and talents – and that is what the *Make your Child Brilliant* journey is all about.

## THE WAY FORWARD

The knowledge held in each of the chapters in this book stems from years of experience. It combines what I have learned from working with thousands of schools, families and children, personal research and the most recent discoveries in brain science, which are continually changing the way we think and learn.

The *Make your Child Brilliant* journey defines the way children can begin to think and learn, so that they not only have dreams, but with the guidance you can provide for them, they gain the knowledge they need to make those dreams a reality. The information in this book is for every child, girl or boy, whatever their age.

No child deserves anything less than the best. I therefore dedicate this book to the success, health and happiness of both you and your child. Your journey towards brilliance starts now.

10 **Your child is brilliant**
Journey's end, journey's beginning

9 **Living and learning**
Making every day count!

8 **Brilliant work space**
Where brain training and focus meet

7 **Goal setting and achieving**
Teaching your child how to succeed

6 **Working with schools**
Cultivating the foundation for your child's future

5 **Getting the best out of schools**
What to look for beyond the 'tourist route'

4 **Cutting tests down to size**
What every parent should know

3 **How your child learns best**
Different ways of learning

2 **Discovering your child's gifts**
Uncovering hidden treasures

# 1 Inside your child's brain
## Understanding the technology

# 1

Two questions occupy the frontiers of science today: what are the infinite possibilities of the human mind and what are the infinite possibilities of the universe? It is both a quirky and beautiful coincidence that these two areas of science have one brilliant fact in common – there are thought to be 100 billion brain cells in the human brain, which is as many stars as there are estimated to be in the universe. In recent years, brain science (also known as neuroscience) has turned a massive corner. Brain imaging techniques, such as magnetic resonance imaging (MRI) and electroencephalography (EEG), enable us to see for the first time cognitive functions at work inside the human brain. For example, computer modelling of neural networks affords insight into how the human brain may process information.

These advances in neuroscience are working to reveal unexplored mysteries of the human brain. They give us a greater insight into how, for example, children's brains process language and deal with other cognitive processes, such as mathematics and problem solving.

You have probably seen images and snippets of information about such research in the popular media. But what you probably don't know is just how much this kind of research has challenged many of the cornerstones that lie beneath long-held assumptions about how the human brain thinks, learns and processes information. There are, therefore, important implications in this research for how today's children are taught to think and learn.

This knowledge is so important that I believe every person should have access to it, and in particular children. Ask children about their MP3, PC or DVD player and they will very likely be able to tell you everything about it, but most children will draw a blank when it comes to knowing about the most brilliant and cutting-edge piece of technology that they are ever likely to encounter: their own brain.

Life is fast paced. Parents that I work with worldwide all have one thing in common: they are working hard for their children and so are understandably busy. This means that, as a parent, in between the school run, holding down a job and bringing home the bacon, you don't always have the time to keep ahead of key brain research that can benefit your child – that's my job. In this chapter, I give you that information in a fast, accessible and friendly manner to keep you and your child up to date. Having some basic brain knowledge is the first step that every child should take in order to maximize upon and realize their individual gifts and talents.

## THE DIY FAMILY BRAIN COURSE

When I am working with children, I like to explain it like this. Imagine you had just bought a fantastic home PC but it hadn't come with any instructions. There may be some great features you could use, if only you could find the instructions and knew how they worked. The DIY family basic brain course in this chapter is here therefore to bring you the facts and features about your child's brain. It lets you get inside your child's brain and at the same time shows them the greatest gift of all: the power of their own brain.

When you have finished this chapter you and your child will be experts in:

★ Important facts and features relating to the brain.

★ How to train your brain to learn new facts quickly and effectively.

★ How to develop higher levels of thinking.

★ Understanding neural nets – the way the brain actually works.

★ How to use everyday activities to tone your brain.

*The 21st century is the age of the brain. On the one hand, it is great that the science of understanding the brain has moved on with unprecedented rapidity in recent years. On the other hand, whenever a parent asks me about my work – be it in New York, Shanghai, London or Sydney – there is always a key question they want to ask: "Can I teach my child to use their brain better?" The answer is, of course, yes. The next question I get asked is: "Don't children find it difficult to learn about something as complex as the brain?" The answer is more simple than they ever expect: a resounding yes. This is because children don't know that something is complex unless you tell them it is. If you teach children about the brain in a fun way and treat it just like any other learning activity, they don't find it complex at all! They just enjoy it.*

*If you look at who is fastest in your house on the PC and DVD, it is likely to be your child. Children are smart. The great thing about children's brains is that they are built to absorb new facts and that includes learning about their own brain. So enjoy the quiz and watch your child learn!*

# Family brain quiz

How much do you already know about your brain?

In each case, circle which fact you and your child think is **True** or **False**

**a** The male and female brain weighs exactly the same **T** or **F**

**b** The corpus callosum is a female brain feature **T** or **F**

**c** The limbic system is important for male and female learning **T** or **F**

**d** Our brains are 60 per cent fat **T** or **F**

**e** As we grow older our brain cells die off and no new cells can be born **T** or **F**

**f** Per minute, our brains use the same amount of electricity that could power a small light bulb **T** or **F**

**g** Brains take up 2 per cent of our body weight **T** or **F**

**h** The right brain takes in sounds and words, but it is the left brain that makes actual sense of it **T** or **F**

**i** Our brains use up 20 per cent of the oxygen we breathe **T** or **F**

**j** Scientists have discovered a heart-brain connection **T** or **F**

**k** Trampolining acts as a brain-toning as well as body toning activity **T** or **F**

**For the answers, see page 160**

# Basic **brain** facts

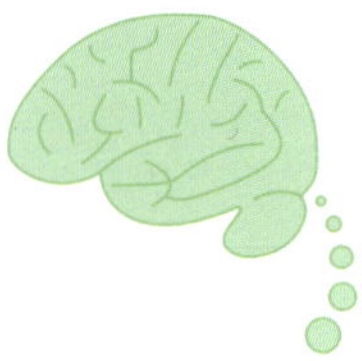

**Brilliant fact!**
Connecting the left and right hemispheres of the brain is a superhighway of connective nerve tissue called the corpus callosum. When children realize the importance of left-right brain connectivity in brain function, they can begin to capitalize on it in their learning.

## THE TRUTH ABOUT MEN AND WOMEN

Our brains are the best state-of-the-art computer to date. Weighing in at 1.25kg for women and 1.35kg for men, the human brain is an amazing organ. And, no, a difference in weight doesn't mean a difference in abilities between men and women. Brain imaging shows that women's and men's brains can process information and solve problems at precisely the same speed, but use the brain differently to do so. The difference is that in both women and men there is a thick band of nerve fibres connecting the left and right brain, known as the corpus callosum, which appears thicker and more pronounced in women than it is in men. The reasons for this are not yet certain, but what we do know is that without this connectivity between the left and right sides, the brain finds it extremely hard to process information.

## LEFT AND RIGHT BRAIN CONNECTIVITY

The right brain and left brain work best for us when they are working together via the corpus callosum. Have you ever woken up to hear the radio in the morning and found you can't get 'that song' out of your head? It is because songs work well to help engage left and right connectivity. At its most basic, the right hemisphere is responsive to tonality, sound, music and rhythm, while the left hemisphere is busy with language processing and rationalizing what it hears. Songs are irresistible to the brain and how the memory works because they activate both the left and right hemispheres, stimulating them to work together. Research has shown that the more we learn how to stimulate left-right brain connectivity, the better learners we become.

> *Secrets of the mind learned: James had Alzheimer's, which was brought on by a stroke. He could hear things but could not always remember what they meant. Then one day someone visiting him decided as a novelty to sing the months of the year to James to remind him that it was June and that it was her birthday. The visitor's name was Janice. Suddenly hearing the months sung to him by his visitor, James was able to remember not only what month it was, but also that his visitor's name was Janice and that she was his niece.*

You might ask how research in Alzheimer's could help us to understand brain development in children. The reason is that by studying damaged neural networks we can learn how healthy brains behave and function. The brain's ability to adapt to damage means that it has tremendous plasticity. This plasticity has also provided an important finding for child development as it suggests that the brain has a tremendous capacity for development and the ability to keep making new connections within and between its brain cells, or neurones. What we are born with is not necessarily set in stone, but can be improved with brain training techniques – and that goes for everyone!

This obviously has implications for how children are taught to use their brains to think and learn. Where children know how

# Left and right brain connectivity

**How the different hemispheres work together to learn.**

This connectivity is one of the most exciting things in neuroscience today. Understanding how the left and right brain work together is one of the key factors in helping children to learn better.

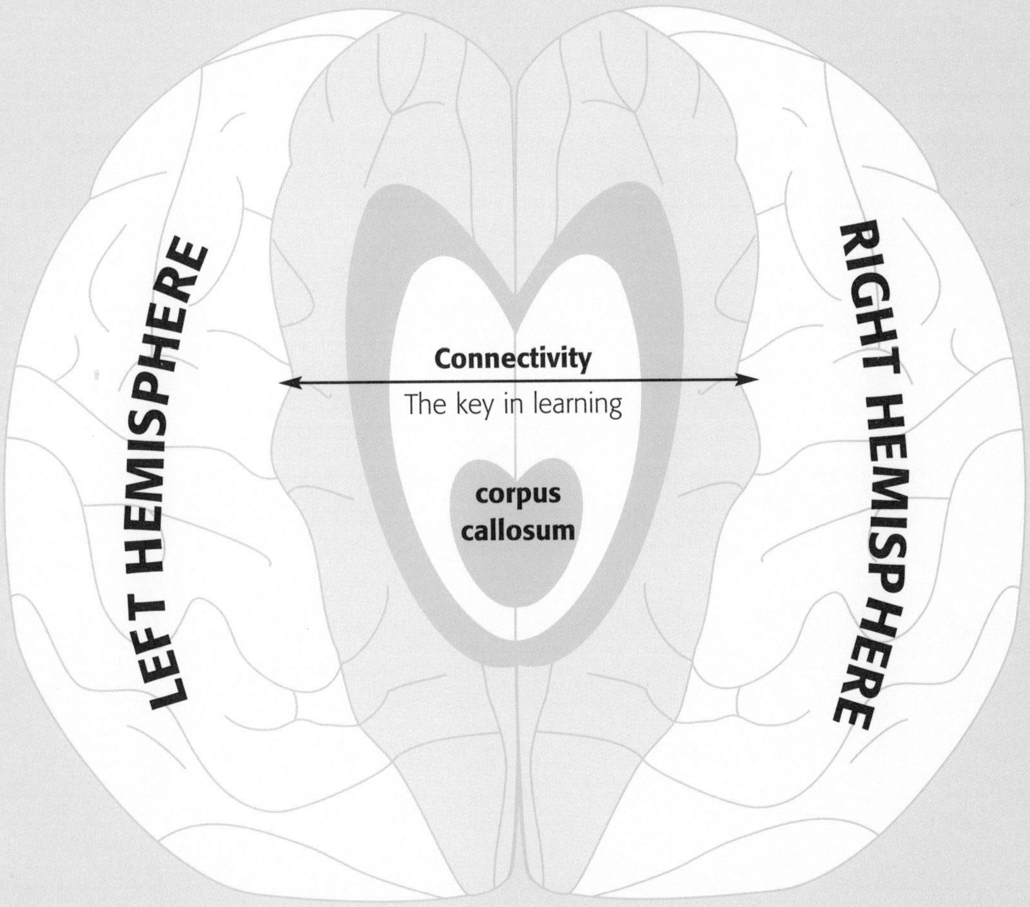


**Left side of brain**

By giving structure and meaning to language, the left side of the brain enables us to understand the words that we read and hear.

**Right side of brain**

Responsive to tonality, sound, rhythm and music, when the right side of the brain hears a word or sentence, it starts processing the message behind the words. Is the speaker trying to tell us something happy, sad or funny? It's not what you say, it's how you say it.

An upbeat and happy tone conveys a positive message.

A downbeat and sarcastic tone conveys a not so positive message.

to develop this connectivity in their thinking and learning, they are on to an instant winner and during this chapter you will be introduced to lots of activities to help your child do exactly that.

James's case study also illustrates the power and importance of left-right brain connectivity in brain function. Only recently has the full extent of this left-right brain connectivity begun to be understood. Traditionally, psychology and child development had emphasized a division of responsibilities in the human brain; with, for example, mathematical and linguistic ability designated a left brain function, and creativity a right brain function. This then led to an assertion that people were right brain or left brain thinkers.

However, brain imaging experiments now reveal that when, for example, children who are confident with mathematics and problem solving are working through different questions, their brain activity is not restricted to either hemisphere. More able mathematicians can be seen using different parts of the brain, to come up with answers quickly and efficiently.

**Brilliant fact!**
From studies in neuroscience it appears that children who are more able mathematicians are using both left and right hemispheres to achieve their answers quickly and efficiently.

Viewed together with the case study of James and others like them in neuroscience today, the findings work to suggest that there is a difference between how the brain may appear structurally and how it may actually operate.

On the surface, the brain appears to have neat and separate compartments. But increasingly the research shows that the secrets of how the brain functions reside not so much in compartmentalization, but understanding the plasticity of the brain and the connectivity within and between different parts of the brain and the neurones that make up its brilliance.

The implications of this wider research in case studies like that of James within neuroscience are exciting for understanding how children can learn more efficiently and maximize upon their brain capacity far better than has been possible in past generations.

★ When children know the simple fact that connectivity best describes how their brain works naturally to learn and process new information, they can begin to use it.

★ Where children are provided with techniques to show them how, they can learn how to grow and develop this natural connectivity and, in the process, become more effective learners.

★ Knowing how to work with this phenomenal natural power of their own brain can really help children get the most out of their learning, both inside and outside of school.

The activity 'Connecting both sides of the brain', opposite, is a great way for children to learn about the importance of this connectivity in their learning, and it is really easy to do.

## THE HEART-BRAIN CONNECTION

It may now be true that if your heart isn't in it, you don't find it easy to learn. Such is the nature of recent findings by scientists that it may begin to put to an end the belief that there is any logic to telling our children to 'think with your head not your heart'. In reality, that just may not be possible for us humans to do.

One of the most amazing findings in recent years crosses the fields of heart surgery and brain science. It seems that for centuries, research may have overlooked one of the biggest connections in the human body between two of its key organs: our heart and our brain. When you think

# Connecting both sides of the brain

**You will need:** face paint

**1** Let your child have a look at the illustration of the left and right brain on page 13.

**2** Let your child loose with the face paints to create one of the faces shown above. The letters act as a reminder that there is a left (L) and a right (R) side to the brain. They are joined together by the corpus callosum (CC).

**3** Ask your child to pick any song and sing it. When finished, explain that it is possible to remember the song because the left and right sides of the brain were being used together. The music and rhythm also helped this to happen.

**4** Tell your child that there are exercises that make it easier to think better and faster, because they get the left and right brain working together. For example, ask your child to try to draw a cat first with the hand normally used, then with the other hand. Explain that this is waking up both sides of the brain, because it is having to do something it doesn't normally do! Now both of you try to rub your tummies while patting your heads. This makes both sides of your brain work together – and it is funny to do.

**5** Give your child the following words to put to a tune that your child thinks fits; it could be a simple childhood nursery rhyme tune, a pop song or anything that has rhythm – even a made-up one. Either way, the main point is that your child thinks about it and, in the process, has some fun.

**Left and right brain make me bright,**
**Left brain works better when it works with the right!**
**Music and rhyme help them work together,**
**With this brain training I can learn better!**

about it, it makes sense to connect these two organs in research. The body may have different parts to it, but, as we all know, we need all of it to work together for us to function successfully.

And the discovery is? Well – within the heart there is, in effect, a small brain. Just as the brain is built up of special nerve cells, or neurones, the heart has been found to also contain these neurones. So important is this finding that it now appears that the heart can influence brain function and quality. The phrase, 'If your heart isn't in it', therefore takes on a deeper more accurate description as to what may happen between heart and mind when we or our children embark on a new project or set out to learn something new. Indeed, all indications are that to understand the brain and the heart, we have to start thinking about them as not separate entities but being inextricably linked.

This new discovery has important implications for child development in terms of how they are taught to think and learn because it reinforces something that brain science has established for a long time:

★ The most effective learning occurs when we are enjoying ourselves.

This is because rather than thinking about learning as being rational, the way our mind learns and remembers facts mixes both rational and emotional inputs. That is why when I am working with families I stress the importance of making sure that whenever a child isn't happy learning something, it is essential that the parents get to the root of the problem and find out soonest why their child is not enjoying that particular class or subject. If you need to tackle a problem right now, then I suggest that you go to Chapter 6 and then come back to this point after you have sorted out the problem.

## THE LIMBIC SYSTEM

If humans were rational thinkers, uninterrupted by emotion, then it is quite likely that half the world's problems would disappear in an instant and we would never find ourselves screaming at our PC screen, because, well, screaming would just not be in our rational vocabulary. As it is, we do not always see eye-to-eye with computers, so either they have to become more like us or we have to become more like them.

The brain has evolved to mix rationality and emotion to make its decisions, and this impacts how we think and learn. To do this, the brain possesses a huge mixing unit called the limbic system. Within this mixing unit evolves the wonderful equations of the mind that bring together emotions, such as love, and feelings, like pleasure, with rational thoughts. It is from this combination of rational and irrational ideas that we as humans get those wonderful spin-offs called imagination and creativity.

Precisely what role emotion plays in our thinking and learning and imagination cannot be fully measured by science because it is hard to put a number or value on such things. But what is certain, is that when children's emotions are positively engaged – namely they are enjoying themselves and having fun – then whatever topic they are learning will be remembered, stored and retrieved much more efficiently.

**Brilliant fact!**

The saying 'if your heart isn't in it…', now has a scientific basis. It has been discovered that the heart has a small brain within it that has influence over brain function. Thinking with your head, therefore, may not be possible without thinking with your heart at the same time.

**Brilliant fact!**

The brain possesses a huge mixing unit called the limbic system where rational thought meets emotions. It is for this reason that fun learning is the best kind of learning.

# Why we think with our heads *and* our hearts

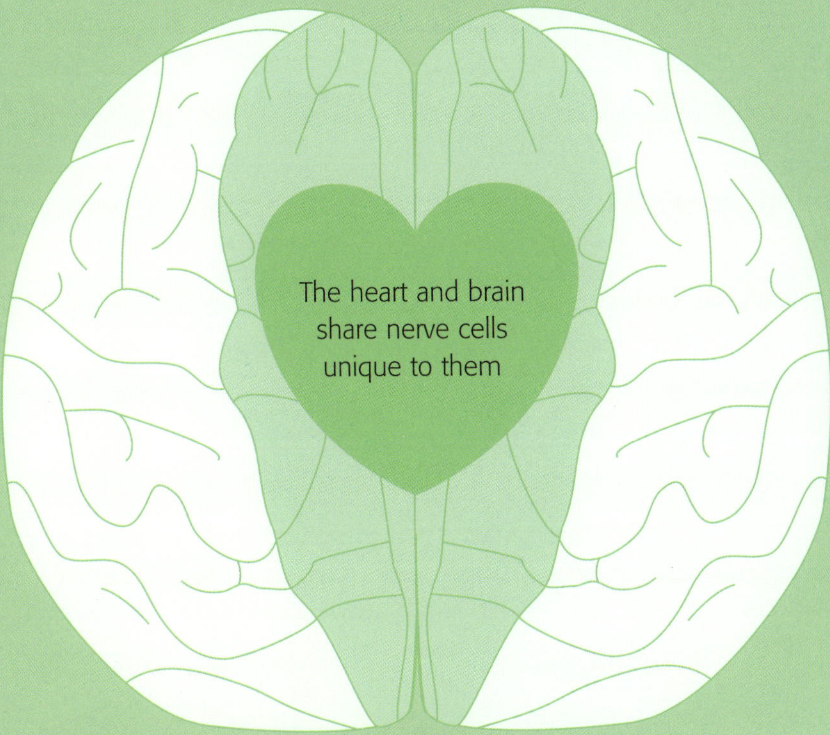


## The heart-brain connection

A new and fascinating discovery that has arisen from the joint ventures of heart surgeons and neuroscientists is that the heart and brain share small cells that are able to interact with one another. This makes the phrase 'Think with your head and not your heart' actually nearly impossible for human beings! And when your heart is in something, you are indeed more likely to succeed, because both brain and heart are working together.

## The limbic system

The limbic system is sometimes known as the mammalian brain. It is a small brain inside our big brain. It houses the pleasure centres of our brain and controls emotions. The limbic system is what in many ways distinguishes us from a computer: we are not rational and linear like a computer, but dynamic, emotional and brilliant human beings.

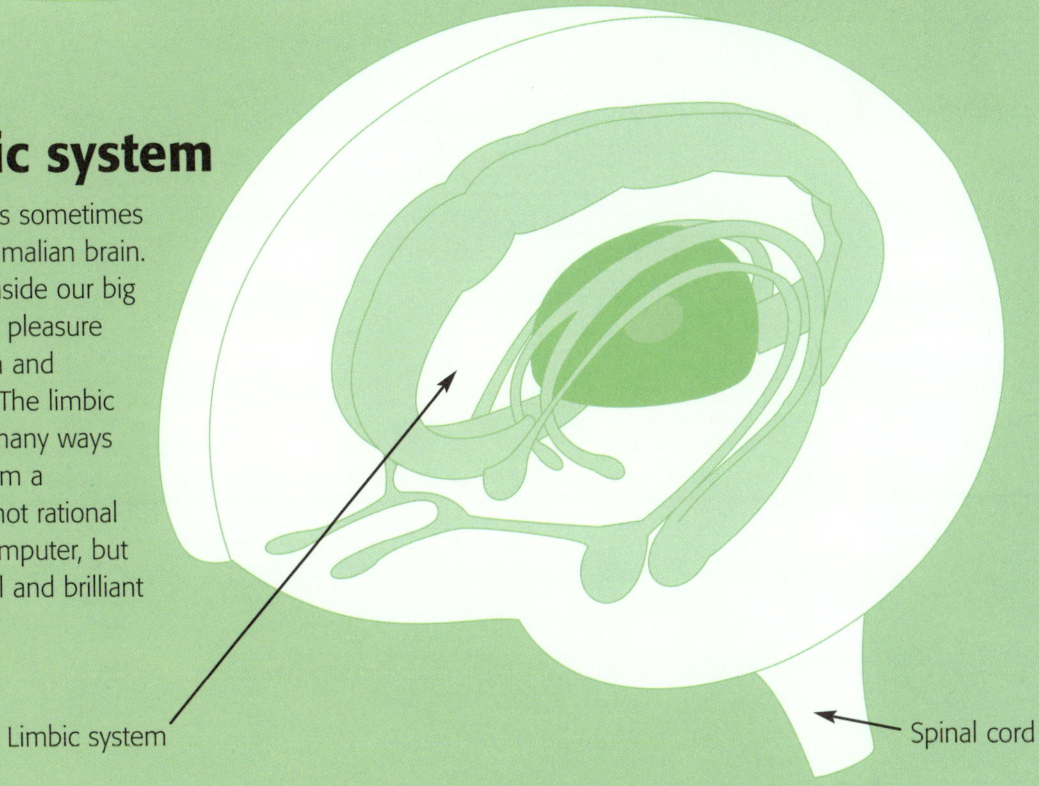

# The engine power that fuels your child's success

You and your child have now learned that the human brain, unlike the best PC or laptop money can buy, is built to withstand damage. It is the personal computer that comes free and standard for all of us with a lifetime guarantee to treat us right, if we treat it right. Forget such myths as, 'As you get older you get dumber'. If the 20th century was all about the fact that we could tone our bodies to keep them fit and young, the 21st century is all about the fact that we can tone both our bodies and our minds; both can be kept fit and young.

One look at the brain facts below lets you and your child see the fabulous natural engine power we are born with. Using the activities in this chapter and the rest of the book shows that if you look after this gift, then it is only you that can put any limits on what you want to achieve. The brain itself knows no limits. Learn that lesson and a new door opens in your child's mind.

So to the heart-brain connection discovery we can add the information that increasingly brain and heart science points to a need to have a balance between the

## Key brain facts

★ Every six minutes your brain uses up approximately the same amount of energy it would take to light a 60-watt light bulb. Every hour, your brain uses as much energy as it would take to light 10 lamps in your home.

★ The brain comprises 60 per cent fatty acids – even when the human body is run down, it always works to retain that all-important fat quotient in the brain.

★ Our brains take up 20 per cent of the oxygen we breathe, but take up only 2 per cent of our overall body weight – making it the best 'portable' computer ever.

★ Once thought to be the case that as we grow older our brain cells die, it has now been found that through a healthy brain diet, new brain cells can be encouraged throughout life. We should:

– regularly challenge our brain to learn new things and think in different ways.

– eat a balanced diet containing omega-3 to maintain the brain's fatty acids.

– take regular exercise to maintain a healthy blood and oxygen supply.

– drink plenty of fresh water to keep mind and body hydrated.

demands we place on our hearts and those that we place on our minds. A happy mind equals a happy body, and vice versa.

## BODY SMART MEANS BRAIN SMART

Many a time in my workshops I get asked by parents about diet when it comes to their children's brain development; in recent years, there has been a lot of information aimed at parents and it can be overwhelming. Basically, all the indications are that a balanced and healthy diet for the body is a healthy diet for the brain too. The old adage healthy body, healthy mind is definitely not a new concept and is just plain old common sense.

What I do advise though, is that given children (particularly as they get to secondary school) are often pressured by peers to go on fad diets and so on, it is important to enable them to understand just what a healthy diet is. For example, they should know about the difference between healthier fatty acids, like omega-3 that you find in fish like mackerel, salmon and tuna, and saturated fats that you find in cheeses and burgers, and that feeding their brain is just as important as feeding their bodies: body smart means being brain smart. Once children understand that having a healthy, balanced and varied diet works for their figure and physique as well as their mind, they get into good habits for life. If at any time, however, you are worried about your child's diet consult your family doctor.

## BRAIN TONING FUN WITH TRAMPOLINING

If you have access to a trampoline, there are some activities for all the family that you can do to tone the brain at the same time as the body (see overleaf). Today, trampolines are a fixture in many a garden. Children bounce around on them for hours, appearing almost addicted to that 'boing', giggling away, as they fly into the air and bounce back down again. It is great fun and anyone can do it.

But trampolining is a unique form of exercise that is not only good for body toning but also brain toning, too. It is so successful that, in fact, trampolining has been used in NASA training for astronauts. No, the reason they used it is not to see how far they can catapult their astronauts into outer space – I am not suggesting that your child is to be the first young person in space launched from your neighbour's

## Metacognition

Metacognition is important in child development. It is the brain's ability to think about how it thinks. That may seem a strange concept, but without this facility our brains would not be able to adapt their thinking to new situations and problems, and view things in different ways. Metacognition is a brain phenomenon that can be toned and made stronger when we practise using it. Trampolining is a brilliant activity that can work this brain ability in children, because it is both fun and physical, giving them the opportunity to exercise both their brain and their body.

But developing metacognition is something that you can do any time you ask your child to think about something in a different way. For example, don't feel afraid to set them little thinking challenges when you are out and about. If you are doing DIY in the house, get them involved in thinking about decisions, such as what colours would go with what and why, which furniture would look best in what corner, and so on. If you are driving a long distance on the way to visit somewhere, get them talking about car design or even road design – how could we do things better?

The great thing is that children are born with fresh ideas and viewpoints. When you engage children in conversation so that they have to use their minds to think about things in different ways, you are helping them to develop their natural metacognitive ability, and what is more, it costs absolutely nothing and is great fun.

trampoline! All very exciting, but this is not what the activities described opposite are about. What is brilliant about trampolining is that it successfully brings together brain and body toning:

★ It works major muscle groups in the body against gravity.

★ It encourages metacognition (see page 19).

To get the most brain toning out of trampolining requires thinking about it as not just simply jumping up and down. For trampolining to work as a brain-toning exercise you need to think about how hard it is to try to land in exactly the same place you set off from. Have a go and you will find that you can't look down, or else you fall over. Your mind needs to think hard and concentrate to take all of your body mass and different muscle groups up against gravity and then bring all of that down again safely in exactly the same place. It is when the brain is thinking about how best to do this, particularly when you keep changing positions to keep it working, that the brain toning really kicks in.

*Aaron was finding it hard to focus when it came to homework. He would often get frustrated and this led to a repetitive cycle where the more he got frustrated, the less he could do his homework. Learning how to use the trampoline not only got rid of excess tension when he first got home from school, it also helped him get in the right state of mind ready to focus and do his homework in a more calm state.*

*During the homework, at 45-minute intervals or whenever he felt his focus beginning to decline, he then learned to break the cycle his mind was forming of getting frustrated and shutting down, by taking a break and trampolining again. He would work out on the trampoline just for a few minutes, come back inside and drink a glass of water to ensure his mind and body were fully hydrated, which also aided his concentration. Then, with his mind back into sharp focus, he would get on with his homework. Using this technique changed the way he approached homework and helped change his routine for the better.*

Like the best ideas, trampolining works because it is so simple and easy for everyone to use. Remember that these results are not just for children but adults too.

Trampolining is a great way also for children to chill down as well as get their mind ready for homework when they have had a hard day at school.

*I was in my local store getting some groceries when a little girl came in with her dad. He had just collected her from the local school and she was feeling really wound up about her day. Her voice was raised as she explained she was all "tested out". Visibly flustered at having sat through a battery of tests, she began rubbing her forehead with her hands, much like an adult might do after a hard day at the office. She turned to her dad and said wearily, "I need some sweets now, Dad!".*

With the pressures children are under these days at school, expecting them to just sit down and do their homework right away can be a little bit like asking us to write a report straight after we did a 12-hour day. A simple exercise like trampolining doesn't take too much time, but can make all the difference for children to get them in the right frame of mind for homework. And if you ever find yourself wound up after a hard day at work, then get on there with them – why not? It is good for you, too!

# Using a trampoline to tone the brain and body

I have devised these activities to help you and your child get the most out of this fabulously fun form of exercise for both body and brain toning – they also help you get the best benefit and value from a trampoline. Always take into account the trampoline size and capacity for safety.

**Activity 1**

This is for one adult and one child (or two children) together. Hold a football between your bodies and try to move slowly clockwise then anticlockwise, while still jumping in the air and trying to keep in the centre of the trampoline. Use the ball as a visual guide to help you.

The object of this activity is not to go higher but to maintain a steady pace and see how well you can do working together. Keep going for 5–10 minutes, taking breaks as feels appropriate.

**Activity 2**

This is for one adult or child at a time. The object of this activity is to challenge yourself to land in alternating positions – sitting down and standing up – and keep landing on the 'X'. You must already be comfortable and practised at landing sitting down or standing up, this is not a physical agility test. Rather, it is to work a mental activity into an already great physical activity to tone the brain. Keep going for 5–10 minutes, taking breaks as feels appropriate.

# Neural nets – how the mind works

Earlier in this chapter I explained that the way the brain stores and retrieves information is not so much localized as dispersed across the brain. What then are the practical implications of this for how children learn new facts? Take the word 'orange', for example. The word could refer either to a fruit or a colour or both. Through experiencing the fruit and its colour, the child learns it can mean both these things. Further, a child may learn that we can use the colour orange as an adjective in association with a great many objects, both living and non-living – an orange coloured tropical fish or bird; an orange bus; the orange in the embers of a glowing fire – and yet still remember that the word orange can refer to something that we eat.

Try to organize and categorize the word 'orange' in your mind and you get headings like: food, fruit, bus, fish, bird, colour and so on. How many different categories you come up with will depend, of course, upon how many connections spring to mind based on your own life experience. For example, orange flowers may spring to your mind in connection with a special day you celebrated and so on.

## MAKING CONNECTIONS

'Connection' is the really important word here. Think about it and the connections any given person can make to the word 'orange' are complex. And whether those connections are lengthy or short, one thing stands out: headings and categories are useful to help us organize our memory. So that we know which meaning of 'orange' to use, massive levels of connectivity between different parcels of stored information in our brains come into play.

Whenever the brain is challenged to learn new facts, it tries to make a connection between what it already knows and the new information it is trying to learn and remember. In this way, it starts to build up an extensive neural network.

But when the brain feels overwhelmed with new facts, it can find all this too much like hard work. At such times its reaction is a bit like if you dipped a large fisherman's net into a sea brimming with all manner of sea creatures. When you pulled the net back out of the sea, all sorts of things would be caught across its length. Some of them you might want, others you may not, but everything would be scattered in an unordered fashion, making it difficult to know what indeed you had caught.

Think back to when you last had to listen or learn something; it might, for example, have been watching the evening news to find out what happened that day. Even though you are watching the news to find out the daily events, your mind will be taking in other information. What about that suit the newsreader is wearing; do you like it? What about the newsreader's hair; do you approve? When it comes to children learning in class, they have the same amount of distractions, plus a barrage of new facts to deal with practically ever hour.

## EXPLORING NEURAL NETWORKS

For children to make the best use of their brains, they need to know how to take charge of them. To do that, the first step is for children to understand that the brain is a brilliant neural network that needs to be managed, so that they can learn better, faster and more effectively. With the techniques and activities in this book, children can learn to do exactly that, and in the process they will also find out that learning about new facts and new topics need not be boring; it can be easy and fun.

Look at 'Building a neural network', overleaf. This shows your child how to turn random facts like sea creatures caught in a fishing net into a 'neural net'. First, your child takes charge by finding the anchor point – the fact that links the species. In this case: oxygen. Species can now be grouped, making learning easier. Why? Because your child is now using their brain's natural neural networks and connectivity to take charge of the information. Using coloured string and card labels to make connections, as suggested in the activity, is not only more fun that just writing a list. It is more effective learning.

In everyday practical terms, your child can do the same thing using a piece of paper and coloured pens to make the headings and connections. The size and dimension of the activity don't matter. What is important is the concept. Once children understand how the brain works, they never forget. Their brain works from this new information, enabling them to think about their learning from a new perspective. And that can only benefit them in the long as well as the short term.

## LEARNING BETTER THAN ROTE

Another technique that works with the connectivity in our brain's neural networks is story telling. By using an invented character or anchor around which a story is built, several unrelated facts or objects are easier to remember. The anchor character unites all the unrelated items so that they have a central connection in the child's mind. This enables learning to happen at a deeper level than just rote learning because the story provides a context in which the facts can become embedded in the brain's neural networks. The result is that once facts are learned like this they can last a lot longer in the human memory.

Rote learning doesn't provide much of an anchor for new facts to be learned because it doesn't help children make connections between what they already know and new information they are trying to learn. In other words, rote learning doesn't work with the natural connectivity within the brain's neural networks.

Try the activity for yourself – see 'Anchoring facts in the brain' on pages 26–7 – the more wild and funny the anchor character and their adventures, the more you will find your child can remember. And you can add items, too; you needn't stop at the number of objects given here.

The reason why you remember so much detail by relating facts together in a story is that by having an anchor to lace them together, and a very colourful story line with which to remember both the objects and their numerical order, the brain has several levels at which to store and retrieve the information. The memory is thus deeper and more meaningful than, for example, just trying to remember a list of unrelated facts without a technique that works with the brain's own natural neural pathways.

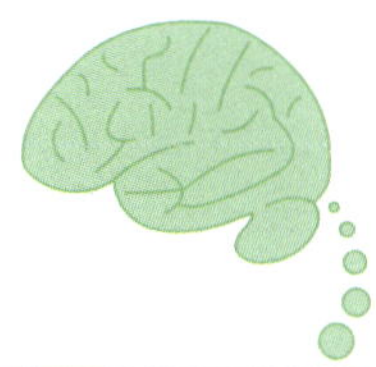

**Brilliant fact!**

Understanding the mind as a neural net is the bedrock of neuroscience. Computer simulations of neural nets, although impressive, are millions of times simpler than what may happen in the brain itself. But once children understand their brains as being a network, they can appreciate that their brains' ability to make new connections is, in fact, limitless! Connectivity counts in learning.

# Building a neural network

The brain is a vast neural network, made up of billions of tiny neurones. Whenever we learn something new, we are encouraging new connections to happen. When children understand that the key to effective and fun learning is knowing how to make the most of this natural connectivity in the brain, they are instantly onto a winner.

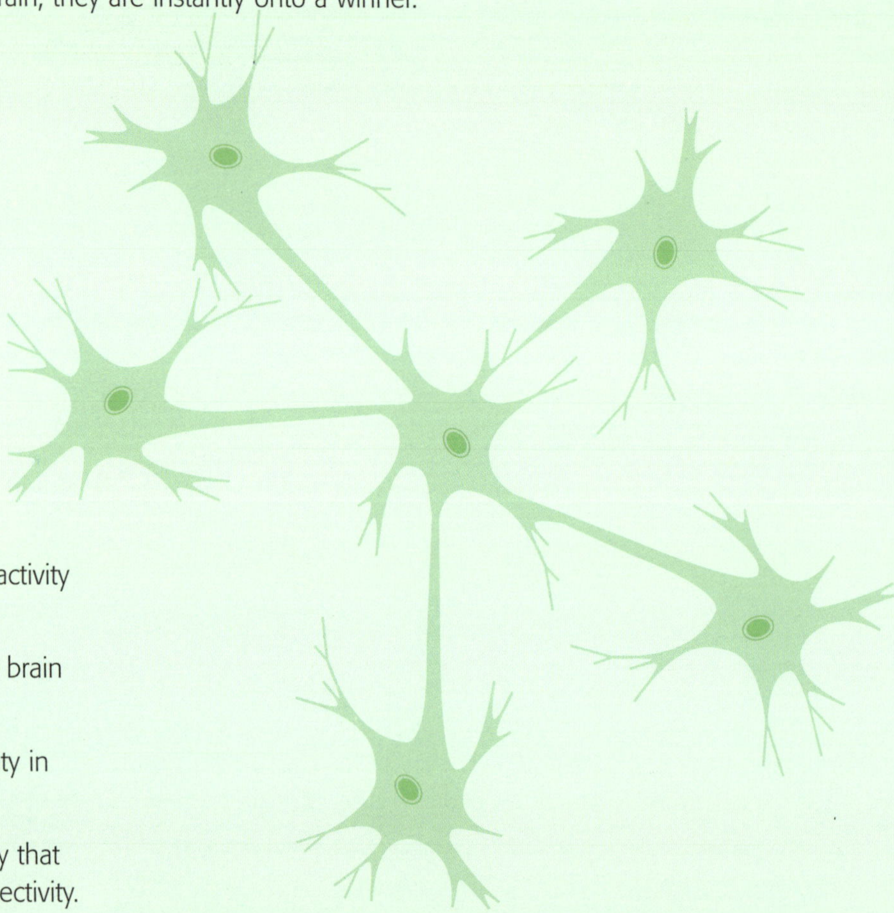

Whenever we encounter something new to learn, the brain is behaving much like a fishing net dipped into the sea. It will pick up loads of different facts, but unless you train it to organize them, you will find it difficult to retrieve or make sense of these new facts.

**Gone fishing**

Here is a really easy brain training activity that helps your child to:

★ Think about and understand the brain as a vast 'net'.

★ Make the most of the connectivity in the brain.

★ Help organize new facts in a way that works with the brain's natural connectivity.

★ Learn a fact organization technique that can be used with a variety of topics.

Start the activity by asking your child to look at the text 'Sea life'.

The problem with the text in the 'Sea life' box is that, as with much factual text, it is packed with information that someone else has organized the way they want it. Passively reading it repeatedly you may take in the facts eventually, but there is a short cut to learning facts like this that is more fun!

**Sea life**

Oxygen is important to many different forms of sea life, whether creatures are warm blooded, cold blooded or don't have any blood at all. Warm-blooded creatures are sometimes called mammals, and include dolphins and whales; these use air holes at the top of their head to breathe. Fish are cold blooded and include small fish, such as sea trout, as well as big fish, such as sharks. They breathe via gills. Creatures that don't have blood still need oxygen to survive. These include, for example, starfish, which breathe through gaps in their skin and tentacles.

**Step 1**: Look again at the text in the 'Sea life' box. Find the common fact or 'anchor' point. In this case it is 'oxygen'; the creatures are different but they all need it.

**Step 2**: Look at the neural net below, which shows how to take charge of the facts, organize them and make them your own. The illustration shows the creatures put into groups around the focal point of 'oxygen'. By doing this, the fact learning is easier, fun and faster.

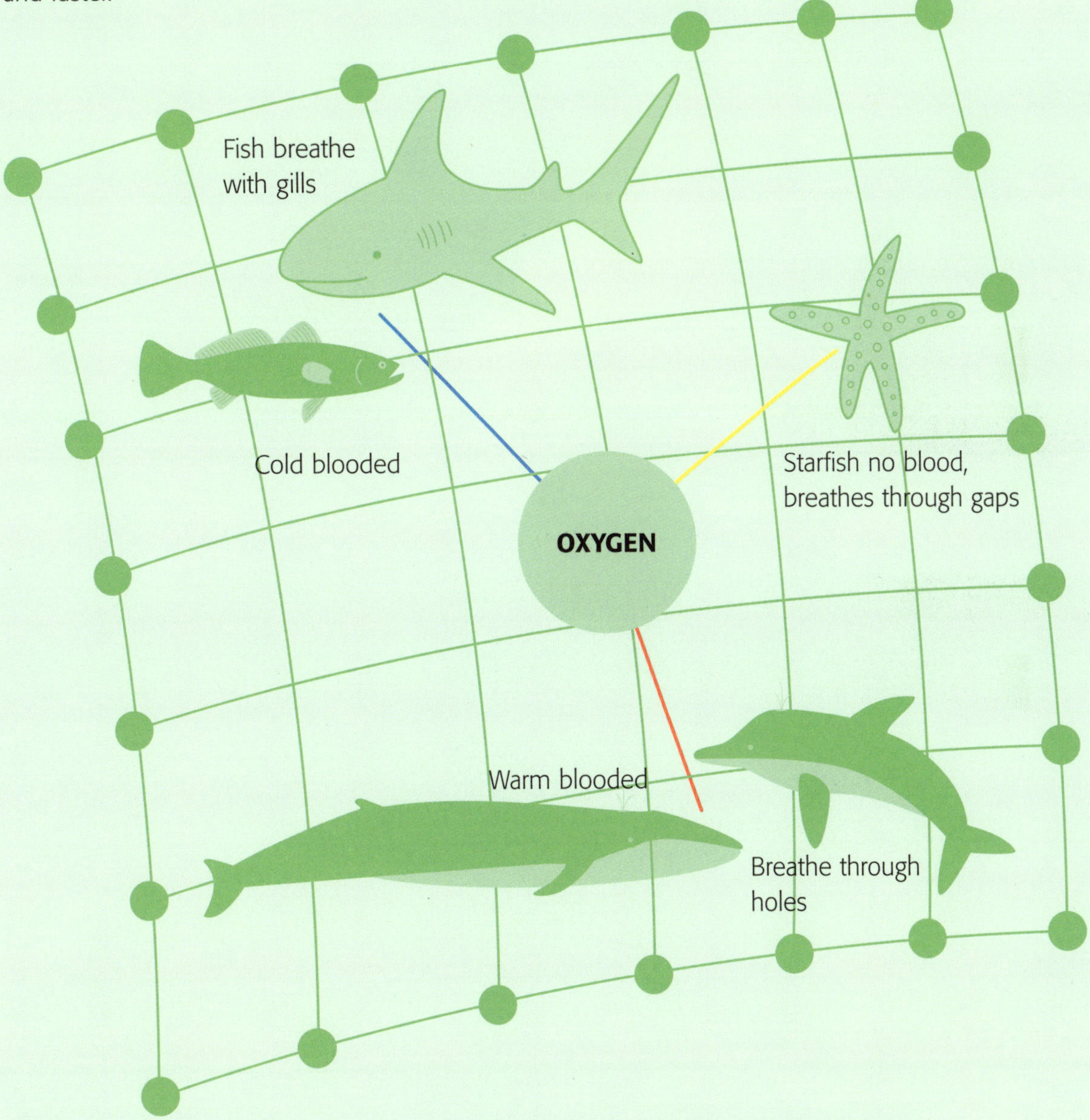


**Step 3**: Now let your child re-create this 'neural net' using drawings of the objects, labels and either different coloured balls of string or felt tip pens to re-create the red, blue and yellow lines. If you and your child are feeling really creative, you can make the creatures out of modelling clay and make a fishing net out of balls of string to create 'a neural net' sea creatures installation for your child's bedroom!

JASPER

CHEESE GRATER

FOOTBALL

## Anchoring facts in the brain

The brain likes anchors to arrange facts around. You have already learned this with the neural nets activity, but anchors can work in a number of ways and in this activity you learn how to use another type: creating eccentric characters in a story to remember unrelated facts or those that are difficult to remember.

Use the story of *Jasper the Eccentric Cat* with your child to see how this works. By the end of the activity your child will be able to remember all of the dissociated objects illustrated above in a precise numerical, but very different, order from that which they are in now.

★ Read or let your child read this story. The words in square brackets are to be enacted by whoever is reading the story. If you don't have the specific objects around the house, you could use different ones, replacing, for example, the panda toy with another teddy bear.

★ Read and act through the story again a couple of times.

★ Let your child draw the different objects in the story and give them numbers too, if that is what your child would like to do.

★ Then go through the story without notes.

★ When you have remembered it, set the story to one side, but go back to it in a couple of weeks' time and test yourself again. You will be amazed how much detail you will remember.

CANDLE

LARGE SPOON

PANDA TEDDY BEAR

PAIR OF TRAINERS

**Jasper the Eccentric Cat**

*This is the story of Jasper the very eccentric black and white cat. Jasper loved playing 'football' [imagine and act out holding a football]. Football was his number one sport [imagine the figure '1' painted on a bright orange football]. Yes, football was his number one sport. Jasper wanted to be better at kicking his football, so he bought a special pair of trainers. He put one on each of his front two paws [lift up your hands and emphasize the word two as you imagine the trainers on them], but they didn't fit him very well and he skidded straight into a wall [act out your two 'paws' skidding into a wall]. Ouch! 'That hurt! I want to go to bed and rest,' said Jasper.*

*When it was time for bed, Jasper had a very special candle at the side of his bed. He had to blow it out not once, not twice, but three times! [Act blowing out the candle, once, twice, three times.]*

*When Jasper woke up in the mornings, he was a greedy cat. He had four spoons of cream [emphasize the word four and act out using the spoon to slurp up cream four times], and five piles of grated cheese [act and count out grating five piles of cheese].*

*Jasper was then ready to play with his pet panda called 'Lucky Six', because he bought the Panda on the sixth day of the sixth month of the year.*

# Never say **no:** there are **no limits** to a **child's thinking**

We may put limits on ourselves, but the brain is not built to have any real limits at all. Via the kinds of brain training you and your child will be learning when you work through this book, you will discover that your brains are absolutely capable of developing higher-level thinking. And the great thing about the brain is that whenever it learns something new, it never forgets that knowledge. With brain training, learnt information comes into play at the moments we least expect it.

## THE BRAIN AND HIGHER-LEVEL THINKING

Within the brain it is thought that there are different levels of thinking that we apply to something. Let's take the analogy of baking a cake. When we first bake a cake, we are just thinking at the beginner's level and so we ask ourselves, what ingredients do I need? And we work from a recipe because we don't know what we are doing the first time around.

Then, when we have made one or two cakes, we start to think about the different varieties we have made. We also might begin to experiment a little, bringing into our recipes things we have learned from other recipes. We are no longer beginners – we not only understand how to bake a cake, its main ingredients and so on, we now also understand that we can experiment with some of the ingredients because we know which ones we can play with and which ones are essential to the cake.

Ultimately, we may begin to examine the governing dynamics of the whole cake and its ingredients and even be critical of the first recipe we used, because now we have our own ideas on how we like our cakes, and also what flavours and decorations we find work best for us.

With just a simple activity like this we have trained our brains to think at a higher level. And that is the trick of developing higher-level thinking in our children. Letting them do simple things like this, that they can do at home, engages their brain. By using critical thinking and their own ideas to try things out, children can experiment and see what happens when they add or switch things around in the recipe. It is great fun and if you let your children loose in the kitchen, who knows what cakes you will be eating! A word to the wise, though, no matter what the results taste like, always smile and praise their efforts with perhaps some simple suggestions as to what they might want to try next. If you laugh at what they have created it will send a message to them not to do that again. So reward their higher-level thinking and lavish lots of praise, and the next time they make you something it may also have the bonus point of being innovative *and* edible!

The important point about activities like this is that the minute children are learning to become more critical and analytical about any topic, not just baking a cake, they are demonstrating the brain's capacity for higher-level thinking. And the questions that start all this in children begin with that all-important word: why?

## THE POWER OF 'WHY?' QUESTIONS

The great thing about children, particularly when they have got past the stage where they can take care of the basics of finding the fridge, food and the bathroom and are starting to see that there is a whole bigger, more exciting world out there, is that they start to ask you those wonderful things called 'Why?' questions. Yes, I know that they can occasionally drive you mad because there can sometimes seem no end to them. But the best solution is not to find

## How to manage 'Why?' questions effectively

**STEP 1**

If every time children ask us a question we give them an answer, with even the best answer we are only ever cultivating one kind of learning: downloading information. When a child downloads a fact like that out of context, because of the way the brain network operates, the brain will struggle to file away the information efficiently. The child is then only likely to remember the fact you gave for a short time. So the first step is not to always feel pressured into giving your child the answer.

**STEP 2**

It may feel funny to do this at first, but you will get used to it because it is fun and much more productive in terms of helping your child develop logic, critical and reasoning skills. When your child asks you a question, bounce it back. Gently ask what your child thinks the answer is. For example:

Child: Why do fish have fins, Mum?
Mum: Well, what do you think their fins might be useful for?

**Why it works**

This gets your child's brain working in a much more active way. As soon as children begin to think about things for themselves, their brains bring to bear any information that might be useful.

During such conversations, children will also make new connections between information they hold in their brain and new facts they are learning. For example:

Child: Maybe the fins are part of the fishes' skeleton, maybe that helps them balance and swim through the water ....

The point is that there is no wrong or right answer in all of this, only the journey to reasoning the answer with you for themselves. And if your child wants to find out more, let it happen; it's fine – there is no upper limit to what the brain can learn about anything, especially for a child.

**Brilliant fact!**
'Why?' helps engage children in higher-level thinking. Nurture 'why?' questions and you are quite literally helping your child to grow their brain.

an end to them, but a way to manage them so that you don't have to feel pressured into thinking you have to be the Encyclopaedia Britannica to get through the day. 'Why?' questions are not only the greatest gift children possess with which to grow their brain, they are also key to developing and nurturing higher-order thinking skills throughout their school years and life.

In 'How to manage "Why?" questions effectively' (see page 29), I show you how to turn 'Why?' questions into an activity that encourages children to use their curiosity, logic and reasoning to figure things out for themselves. With regular practice, this technique can help children develop the analytical skills of higher-order thinking. Remember those neural networks we discussed earlier? To make the most of any new information it is learning, and in order to remember it better, the brain needs to be able to make sense of new information by connecting it back to what it already knows, which is just what this technique does. And furthermore, the beauty of it is that you can do it anywhere – in the car, at the breakfast bar, in the zoo, at the supermarket (on certain busy days of the week the last two places may feel interchangeable!), in the park and so on.

## Unlocking the power of natural curiosity

Curiosity did not kill the cat, it made it smarter. Any time your child comes across something new to think and learn about, gently remind them how their brain's power of curiosity can be unlocked to help them learn about absolutely anything. Engaging this curiosity enables your child to attack a new topic from a number of different angles. When children learn to do this they are helping their brain find a way into any subject. The secret? All your child needs to do to get a route inside any topic is to ask one or any combination of six simple but powerful words that their brain loves:

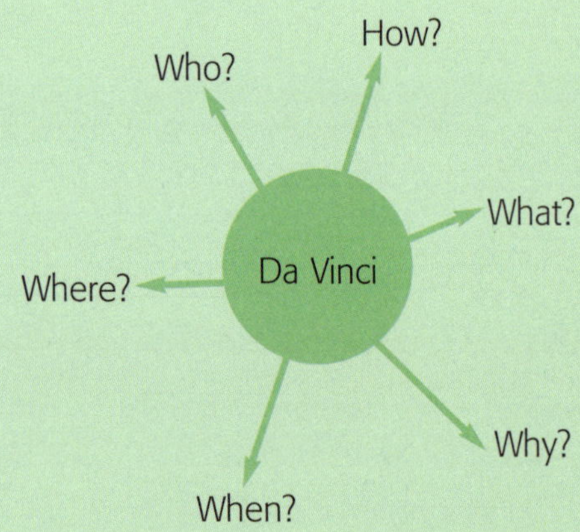


- ★ How?
- ★ What?
- ★ Why?
- ★ When?
- ★ Where?
- ★ Who?

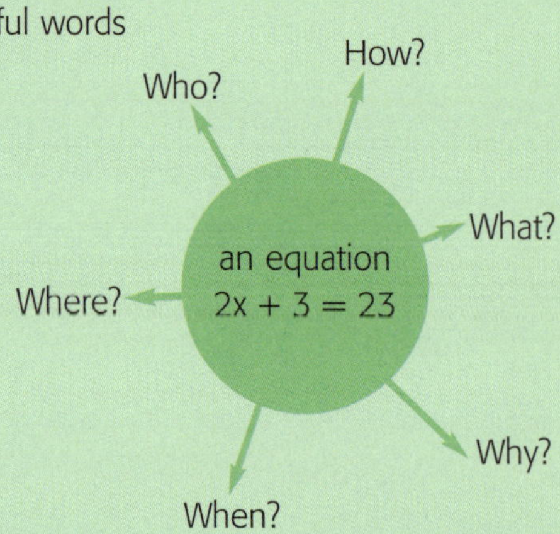

## MAINTAINING A HIGHER LEVEL OF THINKING

Every child goes through a period where they ask lots of 'Why?' questions and are very uninhibited for the duration of this period in their development. But then there comes a time when the intensity of 'Why?' questions starts to dwindle. The trick to developing and maintaining higher-level thinking is to ensure that children never lose the art of asking those all-important 'Why?' questions.

Initially, it may be that managing such questions using the technique in this chapter is your main priority. However, over a period of time, practice in how to use 'Why?' questions becomes a very important skill for children to cultivate throughout their education. Asking these questions can enable children to think about school projects and assignments in original ways, because it trains their mind to think analytically, rationally and critically. 'Unlocking the power of natural curiosity', below, is a simple activity that you can use with your child as a reminder of the joy and power of using natural curiosity to develop higher-level thinking.

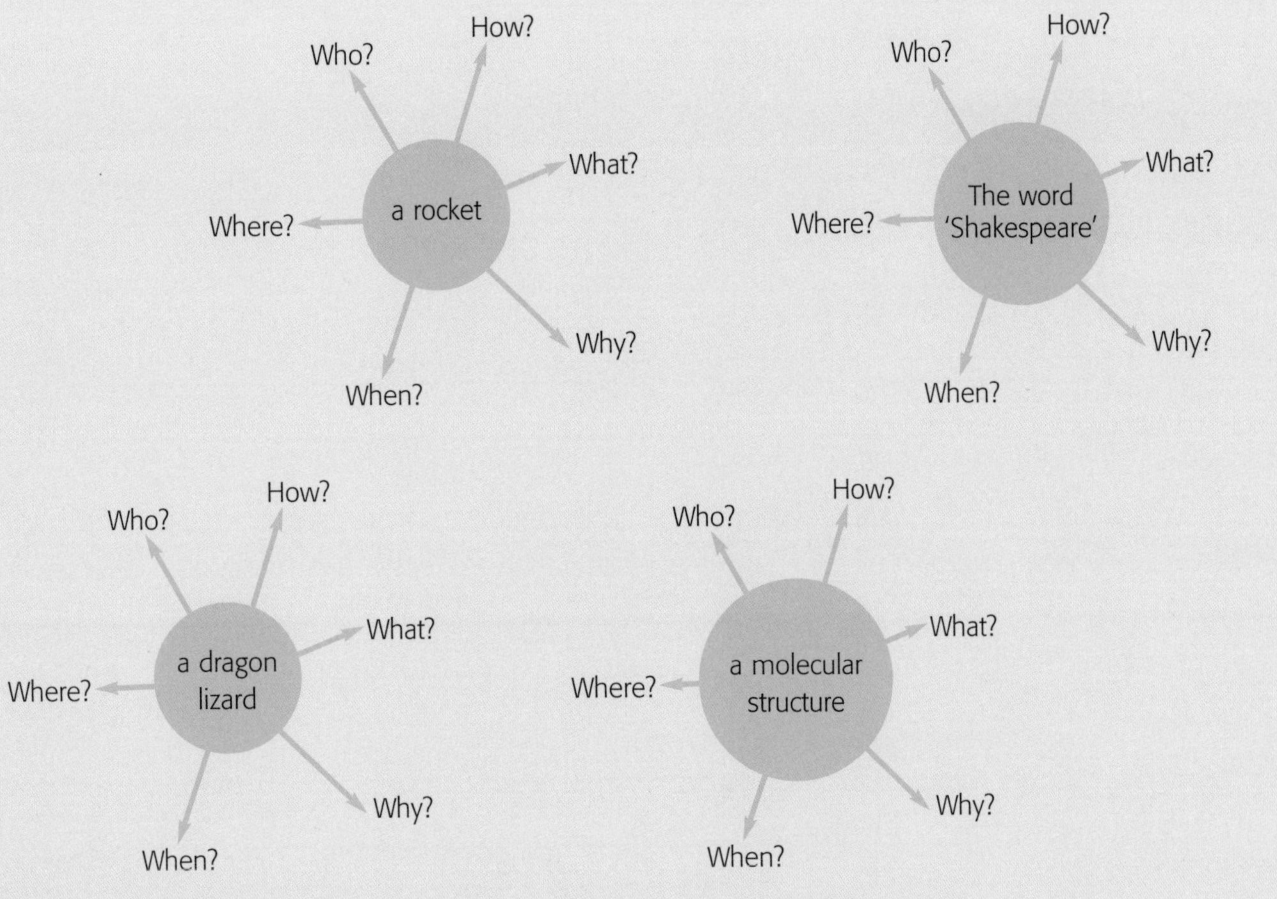

# The **route** to **success** 1

Everything you and your child have learned in this chapter provides the first step in mapping out a route to success with your child. It is the all-important foundation of knowledge about the human brain in child development. Once children have the knowledge that they have learned here, it opens up new possibilities for them, as they begin to realize the brilliance of their brain and how they can bring that power to bear in their everyday world. Every child is special and has individual gifts and talents; the next step is learning how to discover and develop these.

1 **Learn from neuroscience.** New discoveries about the human brain challenge as well as reiterate established assumptions about the way it works. One of the discoveries from neuroscience is the tremendous plasticity of the brain. This has important implications for child development.

Visit the 'DIY Family Brain Course' and the quiz on pages 10–11 and then read the case study on page 12 to find out what research tells us about the brain.

2 **Think connectivity when you think about the human brain.** The brain may appear as separate compartments, but connectivity is what it is actually all about.

See the Brilliant facts! on pages 12 and 14 and 'Left and right brain connectivity' on page 13 to find out about the importance of connectivity in the brain for children. Then let them do the activity 'Connecting both sides of the brain' on page 15.

3 **Remember the role of emotion in the human brain and learning.** Our brains are not rational like computers; indeed, they are built to mix rational and emotional thoughts.

'Think with your head and not your heart' may not be possible for humans. Visit the first Brilliant fact! on page 16 and 'The heart-brain connection' on page 17 to find out why.

4 **Train your body and your brain together.** A healthy balanced diet is good for the body and the brain.

Discover brain training with something children love. Read 'Brain toning fun with trampolining' on page 19 and do the activity on page 21 with your children. It is great fun and they will have a body and brain workout!

5 **Understand your child's brain as a neural network.** To best understand the brain as it really is, a key concept to grasp is that it is actually one huge neural network.

Visit the Brilliant fact! on page 23 to see how once children understand how the brain works, they know their power to learn is without limits.

6 **Teach children how their brain works and they can realize its power.** Once children understand how the brain works they are ready for brain training techniques that can help them learn better, faster and in a fun way.

Go to 'Building a neural network' on pages 24–5 and 'Anchoring facts in the brain' with Jasper the cat on pages 26–7 to share with your child two great brain training techniques that are fun and easy to do.

7 **Cherish and encourage 'Why?' questions: they are great for brain growth.** Learn the art of managing 'Why?' questions and you have brain training in action!

Read 'How to manage "Why?" questions effectively' on page 29 and share with your child the brain training technique 'Unlocking the power of natural curiosity' on pages 30–1.

# 2 Discovering your child's gifts
## Uncovering hidden treasures

# 2

Helping parents to identify the gifts and talents in their children has been my life's work. Every child is special, and there is nothing as brilliant as seeing children benefit from knowing what they are good at and gaining the confidence and belief in themselves that that knowledge brings. With heads held high, they move forwards with the realization that they are unique individuals. The world is their oyster!

Over the years, my research has never stood still. My methods and approach to identifying children's gifts move forward as new knowledge is discovered. For example, recent research now suggests that the DNA we are born with has the ability to adapt to our environment. Such discoveries reinforce the idea in brain and child development that it is not only what gifts children are born with that count, but also the opportunities afforded to them to develop those gifts in their immediate environment.

A question I am often asked by parents when they are looking to discover and support their child's gifts is to what extent can they expect their child's abilities to be genetic. On the one hand, all of us are made up of the gene pool fed into our DNA, but it would be a mistake to think that if you were good at something, then your child will be an exact carbon copy. The way nature deals out its genetic cards is often more complex than that.

# Identifying **brilliance**

Notwithstanding who our parents are, every one of us is born a unique and original person. It is not unusual to find that a child is good at something that neither parent can trace in their immediate family tree. Take the case of Lenny.

*Lenny's parents were a bit concerned about their son. Up to the age of five he didn't seem to talk a lot. Then, by chance, a visitor came to the house and dropped an object on the floor in front of Lenny. It was a life-changing moment for Lenny and his parents. The object was a compass showing north, south, east and west. Lenny was fascinated with it, so much so that it was to trigger a passion for science that was to last a lifetime.*

*Lenny's parents were not particularly gifted in science. Recognizing this, they supported their son by finding him mentors among family relatives and friends that could help him develop his gifts. Lenny's ability in science grew to be extraordinary, and despite some initial setbacks getting into university, with persistence and perseverance he was finally accepted.*

*The rest, as they say, is history. Lenny was to change the way we think and learn about science forever, because he was, in fact, Albert Einstein. Brilliance begins in ordinary homes and ordinary families, with parents doing what they can to support and help their children.*

## DNA

Recent discoveries suggest that the DNA we are born with has the in-built ability to adapt to its environment.

I often use the case study of 'Lenny' when I am working with parents because within it are a few key points that are important when we are looking to discover and develop a child's gifts.

★ Einstein's parents *recognized* that their son was good at something they may not be especially good at themselves; they accepted it and worked with it. This was one of the keys to Einstein's overall success.

★ Einstein and his parents *valued* what he was good at. This can only have set up a positive cycle of thought, which helped Einstein overcome the obstacles that lay between him and his dream.

Contrary to popular myth, it wasn't all plain sailing for either Einstein or his parents. Einstein may have had a gift, but he also had to work at it, have patience and get over rejection and persist before he got to where he wanted to go. I have had the privilege of reading the content of letters that Einstein wrote whenever he encountered a setback. Within the letters is a passion to succeed, no matter how long it would take him. Einstein was not one to flatter his gifts; in fact he was practical about how to achieve his ambition. In his writings he often roots his success in tenacity rather than any special ability.

I have studied what has made people brilliant in different given fields. Popular media often portrays such people as being lucky or having one special gift that made them stand out and so, 'Hey presto!', open the door to their success. The reality, however, is different. Time and again I have found that brilliance and success in any field arises from a weaving together of many ingredients, the least important of which is luck. Brilliance, in fact, has its roots in the following truths:

## BRILLIANCE TRUTH 1

**A child's gift has to be spotted in order to blossom**

For some people I studied, this was later rather than earlier in life, with many of them having to spend frustrating years before being 'discovered'. In such cases, I wonder how the world may have benefited more from their gifts had they been spotted sooner. The point of this book is that your child needn't have to go through life thinking about 'what might have been'. With this chapter they can start seeing and valuing their special gifts – now.

## BRILLIANCE TRUTH 2

**Brilliance has always had a mentor**

This person could be a family friend, parent, teacher or sibling who has believed in and supported and encouraged the person to believe in their gift. This book puts into your hands all the knowledge you need to do this for your child.

## BRILLIANCE TRUTH 3

**The old adage, 'It isn't where you are from, it's where you are going that counts', was never more true of brilliance**

Brilliance starts in ordinary families in ordinary homes, the world over. Every child has something. Wherever and whoever you are, knowing what to look for in your child is the beginning.

## BRILLIANCE TRUTH 4

**Gifts and clusters of abilities make up the whole brilliance of your child**

Take any person who has excelled in any given field and, certainly, they will have a gift in that area. But of equal importance to their success will be the abilities that they will have harnessed to make those gifts work for them. Traditionally, children's gifts and abilities have been pigeonholed rather than taking their whole person and abilities into account. Studying brilliance has taught me to always look for children's individual gifts as well as the range of abilities that go to make up their unique person as a whole.

If you do this when you are looking to spot your child's gifts, you, too, will find a rainbow of abilities that make up that original person.

> *David Beckham and Donald Trump are two successful people in their respective fields of soccer and entrepreneurship. What marks out David Beckham as a brilliant soccer player is not only his physical agility with the ball, but also the way he works within a team. To do this effectively, at any given moment he has to think, play and run with the ball, deciding at lightning speed how best he can martial the talents of his team, to score that goal. Understanding his team-mates' strengths and how to get the trajectory and angle of the ball right are all happening during split-second calculations he makes in his head. It is a cluster of abilities that quite literally come into play when his team scores a goal.*
>
> *Donald Trump is a successful entrepreneur because he has a sharp eye for what the market wants and delivering products that hit the mark. At the same time, he also has to manage a large staff to ensure they understand and are working to deliver the vision he has for his business. Without harnessing all these abilities towards his goals, his business would not be the success it is. Donald Trump has worked hard to combine a strong business savvy with how to get the best out of his company by understanding and valuing people. His massive success over the years speaks for itself.*

What we see at work here is a dominant gift, such as athletic or entrepreneurial ability, supported by a cluster of abilities that each of these respective people have worked hard to harness and apply in their different fields. Once children are aware of their different gifts and abilities they, too, can learn to do this.

## BRILLIANCE TRUTH 5

### A child's gifts need not fall neatly into one particular area

A flawed but long-held mantra that has been passed down from one generation to the next is that children's gifts should all fall neatly into 'either or' categories. This is most often seen in the great art-maths and sporty versus scientific divides. Within this flawed logic the idea that you can be good at both maths and art, or science and sports is considered near heresy! In fact, myths and rules like this belong most definitely to the Dark Ages. Consider the following case study and it is easy to see why.

> *Imagine for a minute the Harvard and Princeton rowing teams out on a stretch of water in all their finery on a bright and sunny spring day. They are gliding gracefully along the River Charles. Among the rowers there are gifted scientists, artists, musicians, philosophers, mathematicians and linguists. At the same time, in order to be out there representing their university, no one would doubt that all the rowers must also be gifted athletes. In such a case, it is impossible to try and think about the people in these rowing teams in terms of having single as much as interconnected abilities. It is these clusters of gifts that make them – like your child – who they are: each is a unique person with their own special gifts.*

Da Vinci dabbled in mathematics, art and music and, in his day, no one had a problem with this. The only time this kind of 'across the board ability' became an issue was when mass education systems for ease of organization, among other things, resulted in creating synthetic divisions between subjects in their curricula. This happened worldwide and suddenly, around the 19th century, the arts and sciences became firmly divided and were seen as two different planets in mass education, and hence in the minds of children. None of this would have made any sense to Da Vinci and his peers.

Today, though, a renaissance is occurring as disciplines in universities divided over the centuries give way to exciting mergers between fields. Having the opportunity to work across disciplines means that children are now more likely to be able to use the full range of their abilities as they grow and develop, rather than having to think of themselves and their gifts in one-dimensional terms.

*James was interested in art, mathematics, computer games and films from a young age. He could remember detailed accounts from computer games and films. His parents sometimes worried that he appeared dreamy, in a world of his own. When James was in junior school it became clear to his parents that he had a great love of mathematics. But when he moved to secondary school, he then took an interest in art and English literature, and loved swimming too. James had to work on the swimming because initially it wasn't his best ability, but his parents were supportive of his enthusiasm. James remained serious about swimming, winning at county championships.*

*As James entered the final stages of his school career, he returned to his love of mathematics, combining this with art and computers and an avid interest in films. At first, his school was not happy with the diverse range of options James chose, but he succeeded with flying colours, working easily across the disciplines. His parents stood by him. Today James has combined a successful career in law with his own film-making business.*

In the 21st century, increasingly studying across disciplines like this opens up great opportunities for children the world over. The message is simple: go with what your child enjoys and is good at; while also supporting them to develop areas they feel they need help in – prepare to be amazed!

**Brilliant fact!**

When you are looking to discover your child's gifts, don't look to narrow abilities into neat pigeonholes. Think more of abilities as the rings of ripples you get around a rock in a lake. Think child first and then work outwards to discover the possibilities.

**Brilliant fact!**

Being good at mathematics does not make your child necessarily a left-brain thinker, being an artist doesn't necessarily make your child a right-brain creative person – our children can be both because, contrary to popular myth, that is how our brains really work. Being gifted at both mathematics and art, for example, is what makes the best computer games designers.

# Discovering your child's gifts

To discover your child's gifts, cast your net wide. Think beyond how you yourself were classified by school or even your own parents. This may sound radical and slightly irreverent, but the fact is that research in understanding brain development, gifts and abilities has moved on, giving you a massive advantage over past generations. Earlier generations used the best knowledge they had at their fingertips; now you are doing the same thing, only from a vastly better informed vantage point.

So cast your net wide. Look for different indications of gifts in your child from as many different sources as possible, both inside and outside school. Following the carefully structured steps below, you will locate different gifts and layers of ability that will finally interweave, revealing the full range of your child's individual brilliance. No one will ever have done this for your child before and now you can do this together in the comfort of your own home, using the following seven-point plan.

## STEP 1

**Consult your child's national test scores – but don't see them as the be all and end all of your child's gifts, for they are not**

Einstein is once alleged to have said that: 'Not everything that can be counted counts, and not everything that counts can be counted'. He was talking about astrophysics and the gaps left by maths when it comes to understanding fully the universe. But his wisdom could apply equally as well to how children's abilities are measured and quantified in education today. Not every gift a child possesses can be captured on pen and paper tests. If a gift cannot be measured, it makes it no less valuable. Nearly two decades in the field of gifted children has taught me one essential lesson: important gifts that make a child's abilities exceptional can become lost in a sea of national tests. If you know, therefore, how to look beyond test scores to find your child's range of abilities, you stand a better chance of both locating and supporting your child's gifts.

Today's generation of children has endured a phenomenal barrage of tests. Despite political soundings to counter this, the 'death by testing' culture remains strong. Testing tends to narrow the ability search by focusing on 'core' subjects such as literacy and maths. These subjects are important but they act as only one indicator of your child's abilities.

To start finding out more about your child, go to 'My measurable gifts', overleaf, and together think about each of the academic subject areas in which your child may have been tested either in national or class tests. In each case, regardless of the test score (if any), let your child give themselves a score of 1–10 in each subject. Ask your child to be honest and open with you as well as themselves. Make a note of the scores they achieved and your child's

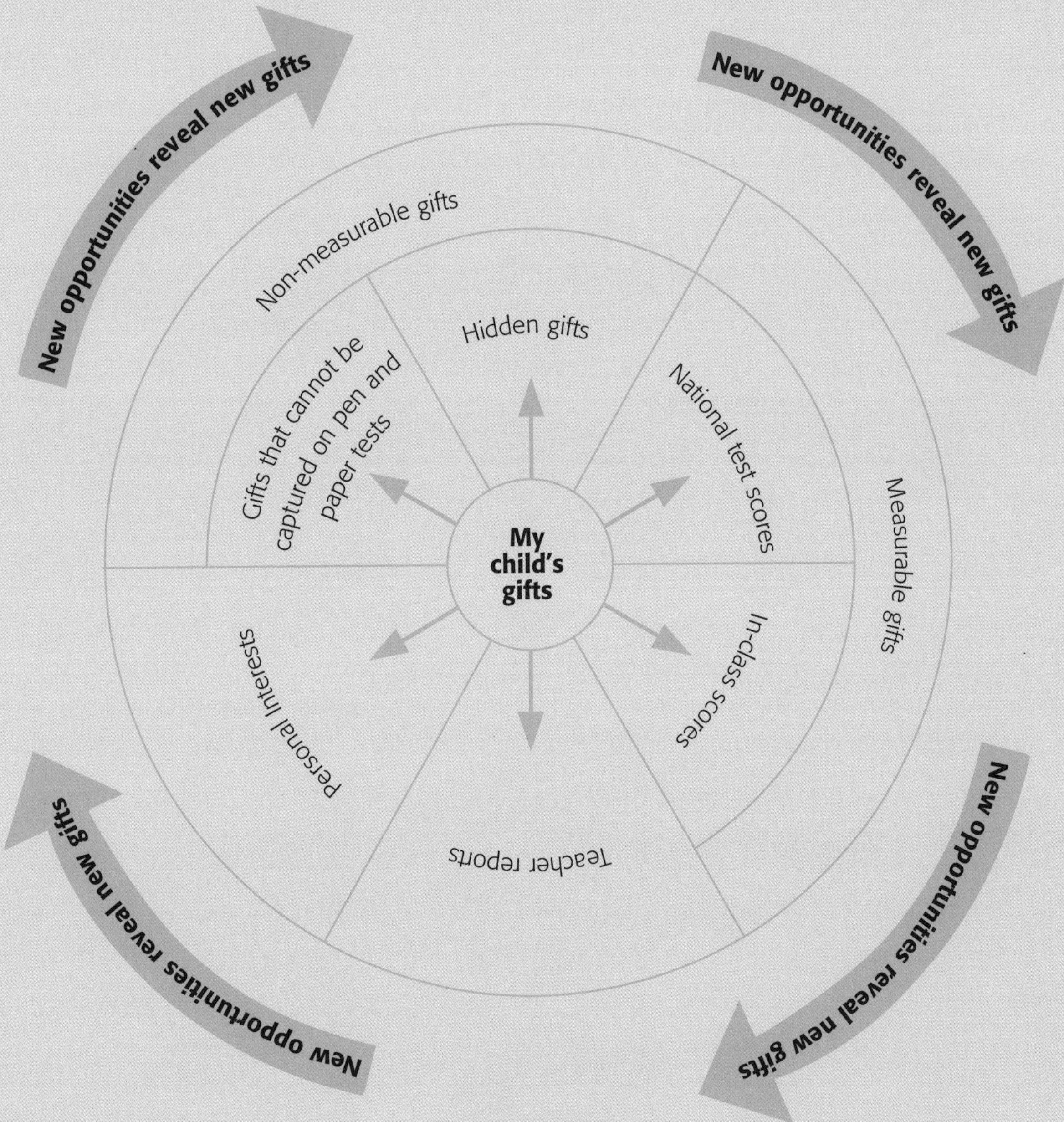


# How to find your child's gifts

This web provides you with an overview of what I do when finding children's individual gifts and talents. The seven-point plan I describe in this chapter is how I work to find each child's unique gifts.

With each step you and your child will be able to get a full sense of their gifts – and at the same time probably find some surprises along the way.

Working through the steps on pages 40–56, it is useful to keep a notebook handy and be prepared to be amazed at how many different abilities and gifts you and your child will find.

The headings on this diagram show how different areas in your child's life overlap to form a unique whole.

Name: ..........................................................................................

# My measurable gifts

| Subject | Test score (if any) | Your mark (1–10) |
|---|---|---|
| English | ______________ | ______________ |
| Mathematics | ______________ | ______________ |
| Science | ______________ | ______________ |
| Languages | ______________ | ______________ |
| – Chinese | ______________ | ______________ |
| – French | ______________ | ______________ |
| – German | ______________ | ______________ |
| – Russian | ______________ | ______________ |
| – Spanish | ______________ | ______________ |
| – Other | ______________ | ______________ |
| Computer Technology | ______________ | ______________ |
| Design | ______________ | ______________ |
| Art | ______________ | ______________ |
| Drama | ______________ | ______________ |
| Music | ______________ | ______________ |
| Sport | ______________ | ______________ |
| Other | ______________ | ______________ |
| Other | ______________ | ______________ |

own view of how good they are at the subject you are discussing. Ask your child gently the following questions:

★ What subjects would you like to be better at?

★ Which subjects do you enjoy and why?

The point here is to find out if there are any areas your child could be good at, if only certain things that were getting in the way were removed. So, when you are discussing these questions, it is important to let your child know that test scores are not the be all and end all of their gifts and that scores can be improved.

To help set up a congenial atmosphere for honesty during the discussion, use the checklist in the 'Honesty box', below, as a guide. Open-ended questions are easier for a child to answer and by setting up a gentle, positive, supportive tone, your child can feel confident and happy discussing each subject area.

One word to the wise: during this 'honesty' discussion, do not put pressure on your child to do better. Pressure never works, it just boils over and backfires, usually ending in a paddy – and your child may get upset too! Neither of you need that. If you feel your child is getting tense about a subject, back off, chill, have a break, come back and let it all come out naturally in their own time.

Apart from discovering gifts, this step provides you with a chance to locate the source of any problems so that you can nip them firmly in the bud.

## The 'tink, tink, tunk' rule – if it doesn't sound right it likely isn't

At this point I have a rule to introduce you to. It crosses all cultural boundaries and works with amazing accuracy every time.

How does the rule work?

★ When things are going well for your child at school, all feedback you get from school and child tallies. All sounds right. That is when you have a 'tink, tink, tink'.

★ When things are not going well for your child, you can't quite put your finger on it, but something doesn't feel quite right. That's when you have a 'tink, tink, tunk'. The information you are getting doesn't tally.

Here is an example of when the 'tink, tink, tunk' rule comes into play. A child was doing well in a subject at the end of last term, then suddenly this term they are nose diving. Something has changed, which is affecting how well they are doing.

If you ever 'hear a tunk' like this, act on it right away. The curriculum moves on fast and time is always of the essence. Let it slide and an opportunity is lost. Get to the root of the problem now, and alert your child's teacher so that your child will be right back on track again.

### Brilliant fact!

If your child doesn't do well in a test, this may not be an indication that your child is not good at that subject. Looked at in a different way, a test result is not just a test of your child's performance, it can also indicate which classes and teachers work to bring out the best in your child and which do not.

## **Honesty box** checklist

✓ What subjects do you think you are really good at?

✓ Why do you think you do well in that/those subjects?

✓ Which subjects do you think you would like to be better in?

✓ Why do you think you are not doing so well in that/those subjects?

✓ What do you think we could do to help sort this out?

## STEP 2

**Look for evidence of gifts beyond 'tests' in teacher reports. Imagination is one of those special gifts that children possess and which cannot be measured, but is very important in many fields**

For example, if you have a budding J.K. Rowling at home, which do you think is going to matter more to a future publisher: how well your child did in a test, or how much imagination is credited to your child's creative writing in the school report? No prizes for guessing the right answer there. Tests can grade literacy but not imagination. A teacher's report will usually cover both and more.

Remember that classroom teachers don't design curricula or national tests, they just deliver them. Therefore, the report card is often the only chance teachers have to relay a range of information about your child's gifts and abilities that are not confined to test scores. Teachers are there 75 per cent of the week with your child and the majority of them want children to succeed, and hence their comments will often provide lots of indications for spotting abilities.

However, what I have also found through working with teachers is that their time these days is often drained away with a mass of paperwork and test documentation. The time taken on such tasks can therefore often detract from the business of what teachers would like to dedicate their time to: spotting individual gifts and talents and helping to develop them.

I have worked with schools to help teachers spot children's gifts because, as you are discovering, they come in all kinds of guises, not all of which are obvious. Sometimes they are quite literally hidden. These gifts are the most difficult to spot of all, and at the same time can be absolutely integral to a child's overall success. For this reason Step 3 is all-important for you and your child.

## **Teacher reports and comments** checklist

✓ Check back over school reports with your child.

✓ Together make a list of any attributes that your child's teacher comments on in school reports.

✓ Are there any patterns you notice in the teacher comments?

✓ What kinds of things regularly seem to feature?

✓ Which subjects seem to be attracting the best comments?

✓ Is there a pattern of comments that seem to highlight certain attributes?

✓ Note anything you and your child notice as you go along.

✓ Finally, make a summary note of all good attributes and negative comments.

## STEP 3

**Discovering your child's hidden gifts**
**Part I: Mistaken identities**

Do you remember the scene in the *Da Vinci Code* where Tom Hanks, playing a professor learned in code cracking, has the clues right there, but he just can't make sense of them to find the hidden treasure? Then suddenly he has a moment of realization. After taking a while to reflect, he finds that the most important clue he was looking for was right there under his nose all the time, and yet he just couldn't see it.

A lot of the time our children's gifts are just like this: right there under our noses. But even if you had the clues in front of you, how would you know what they were or what they meant? For centuries, looking for children's gifts has become an exercise

## Signs of hidden gifts

Brilliance comes in all shapes and forms. One or all of the following things can be a key indicator of a highly developed and quick thinking intellect at work.

★ Brilliance can come in the shape of a low boredom threshold, which is recognized as a key indicator a child may be gifted in one or a variety of subject areas and wants extra challenges to spur on their brain.

★ Gifts can be masked by a quick wit, a highly developed sense of humour, chattiness or just sheer mischief in the classroom. A child may prefer to have a conversation in the company of elders rather than their own immediate peer group and appears precocious, or even cheeky, when doing so.

★ Children don't always 'behave' or develop in the stages that curricula expect them to. They may not want to wait to move on to the next topic; they may have a particularly enquiring, almost nosy, manner. This is a key indicator that the child is thinking in a way that is beyond their years and needs supporting.

that extends only to how well they did on their last test score. But children's gifts are more precious than that; in fact, all children have their own individual gifts waiting to be discovered and developed.

The key point for a child to have their gifts recognized in full, therefore, is to know what to look for in your child. It is all about reading signs that otherwise may pass you by. A simple or cute thing you notice early on could, in fact, hold the key to a whole rich seam of gifts and talents that until now has lain hidden from view.

To discover the full range of your child's gifts and abilities, and get the best out of this step, you and your child need your notebook and pencil. Get yourselves comfy, ready for a journey that will open up many doors to new opportunity for years to come. First, work together through the 'Is this me?' questionnaire, on page 46.

Discuss the findings in each of the areas with your child. Celebrate the areas that your child feels good about. Address any areas they feel they may need to attend to, either to get their gifts more noticed or, for example, if they get bored quickly, think about how teachers can help to rectify that. For example, most teachers will be happy to set extra challenges in class and homework to keep eager minds engaged!

### Boredom: the mask of brilliance

If your child suffers from boredom more often than not and it is happening across subject areas, take this seriously and act fast. When children feel disengaged it gets into a habit and they can adopt one of two strategies to deal with it.

**Brilliant fact!**

If your child is feeling frustrated with a particular subject or topic, then you need to do some sleuthing to find out why that is happening. The best way to do this is by having a gentle, calm and matter of fact conversation with your child, with no pressure but just a gentle prodding to get to the bottom of it.

**Brilliant fact!**

Getting spelling into perspective: Good spelling is great and useful but here is some news that may help you get spelling in context when it comes to thinking about and discovering your child's gifts. Einstein wasn't very good at it and Leonardo Da Vinci may have been dyslexic, because he wrote everything upside down and back to front, so you needn't worry if your child's spelling isn't as good as their ideas. Spelling and intellect are not interdependent. It is great if your child can practise spelling or even become a great speller, but many a brilliant person in many a different field didn't let not being a particularly great speller hold them back. The message for your child: practise spellings and get them right if you can. But also value your imagination and creativity… they are the stuff of greatness in the end.

Name: ..............................................................................................................................................

# Is this me?

**1** Do you ever find in class that you become bored?
If 'yes', say whether the answer is a or b.
If 'no', move on to question 2.
**a** This happens frequently. ☐
**b** It only happens sometimes. ☐

**2** Do you find that there are questions you would often like to ask, but you don't because either:
**a** You might feel silly. ☐
**b** Your peers might think you are being a 'swot'. ☐
**c** You don't think it is of interest to everyone else, so you don't bother. ☐
**d** One, some or combination of all of these reasons. ☐
**e** Any other reason? ☐

**3** Do you ever find homework boring?
If 'yes', say whether the answer is a or b.
If 'no', move on to question 4.
**a** For all subjects. ☐
**b** For some subjects. ☐

**4** Do you sometimes get in trouble in class for …
**a** Chatting? ☐
**b** Playing tricks with friends instead of focusing on your work? ☐
**c** Shouting out answers ahead of time because you can't be bothered waiting? ☐
**d** Doodling or day dreaming? ☐
**e** A combination of one, some or all of these? ☐

**5** Do you find it difficult sometimes to sit still in class, preferring to move around if you can?
**a** Yes. ☐
**b** No. ☐

**6** When you are writing down your ideas, do you prefer to …
**a** Use big words, even though you can't spell them very well? ☐
**b** Focus on your ideas, rather than your punctuation and spelling (this is particularly important if your child is dyslexic)? ☐
**c** Enjoy thinking up stories and being imaginative? ☐
**d** Some or a combination of all of these? ☐

**7** Do you sometimes find that you have the answer to a question way ahead of everyone else?
If 'yes', move on to the question below.
If 'no', move on to question 8.
When this happens, are you …
**a** Fed up so you wait for the others to catch up? ☐
**b** Secretly annoyed with yourself that you knew the answer already and waited? ☐
**c** Glad you waited so that you remain popular with your friends? ☐
**d** One or a combination of all these things? ☐

**8** Do you sometimes find that you prefer talking with older people more than you might your own age group?
**a** Yes. ☐
**b** No. ☐

★ One strategy is to lie low. These children can spend all their school years undetected. They are model students behaviourally and always form the biggest enigma for teachers when they under perform: 'I don't know what happened to their test score, they are so well behaved in class …'

★ Another strategy is to become the class clown. These students are highly popular with their friends and spend a lot of time getting into trouble. Fidget is usually their middle name – after mischief that is!

## The calm and the collected vs the wild and the wonderful

Neither strategy wins for these children. The more 'colourful' characters will get noticed, but for all the wrong reasons. Instead of being recognized for their quick creative thinking, they are more likely to end up in detention. These children, if not spotted, can often tend to excel *after* they have left school in areas such as entrepreneurship, acting, writing or becoming Michelin star chefs! In fact, anything that enables them to use their quick thinking and highly creative brain. They are often the people that especially want their own children to succeed because they would have liked to have learnt more at school themselves.

The calmer character of the two is the kind that endures school with hardly ever getting a detention, who then saunters out of the school gates almost unnoticed to land a job they don't particularly like. Later, often by chance or sheer hard work, they find out how intelligent they are and are doing a PhD in their mid thirties when they could have done it in their early twenties.

The point is that if only someone had spotted their gifts at school, their opportunities may have come sooner.

**Part II: Reading all the signs**

Making sure you have made a note of anything you have already discovered and discussed with your child, you will now be ready to work together through 'Your child's hidden gifts: do you have one of these at home?', overleaf.

The descriptions given on the following pages are designed to show you the ways in which different gifts and clusters of ability can present themselves in children. They are not meant to be a prescriptive or definitive list, rather their purpose is to reveal to you and your child the range of brilliance that can lie hidden unless you know what to look for.

Read through each of the descriptions together, making a note with your child of any attributes that ring true in their case. Instead of trying to fit to any particular description, look for abilities that you and your child identify with, building up your own special portfolio of gifts as you read. As you go along you may add a few attributes and ideas of your own.

Every child is as unique as their own thumbprint. By the time you have reached the end of this step you will have a portfolio of abilities that is designed around your child's own individual gifts.

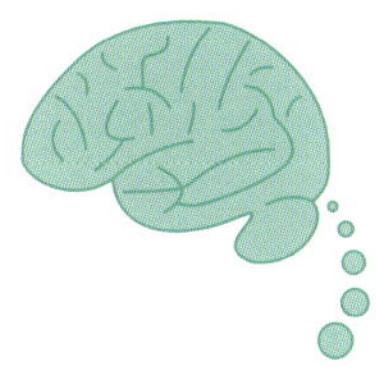

### Brilliant fact!

As you have worked through this chapter, always focus upon and celebrate the positives. One of the easiest things to do as a caring parent is to blame any shortcomings your child may have at school on your own shortcomings when you were at school. It goes a bit like this, 'Oh well, I remember I wasn't that good at x at school either, so it follows my son or daughter is having problems too.' That is a big 'no, no' in the *Make your Child Brilliant* journey. With the best will in the world, it sets up a cycle of negative expectation for children, so that they start to believe it is inevitable that they can't do well on a given subject. And that is poppycock! All healthy children are born with the natural in-built ability to learn absolutely anything. And that's a fact!

# Your child's hidden gifts: do you have one of these at home?

As you are reading through the following descriptions, remember that every child is an original, a one-off. The point of this exercise therefore is not to make your child fit any of these descriptions in particular, although they might ordinarily do so. Rather, as you work through them, keep a tally of any quality that either you or your child thinks rings a bell, and then make a note of these in your notebook as you have done in all previous steps.

## The bossy boots

**What to look for:** These children are not afraid to stand up and be counted, and friends who realize their innate gifts stick by them. Others, however, find their ability a threat and can be jealous. But that rarely bothers the bossy boots because they know they aren't bossy at all but, in reality, have a rare and fantastic gift: the ability to lead and facilitate people, and see problems from different angles, so that a bossy boots brings out the best in any team of people, anywhere.

**Delving deeper:** The bossy boots among us will have arranged their kindergarten play corner within the first hour of arriving on their first day. Later in junior school, they will have reorganized their teacher's seating arrangements on their table, because, well, the way it was before just didn't make good sense. The teacher disagreed initially, but on reflection found 'bossy boots' to be right. If these children play team sports, they are always the leader, not because they are bossy, but because there they can use their abilities to organize the team better, and although not everybody likes this, they do deliver results. In school plays, they usually feature highly as either a narrator, lead actor or sorting out costumes backstage – the teacher knows that with a bossy boots in charge, things get done, so such children naturally get a lot of responsibility and, of course, power.

**In the future:** This combination of gifts is what works to make great captains of industry as well as great captains of sport – indeed, a bossy boots can make it anywhere because with skills like this, everyone wins.

## The code cracker

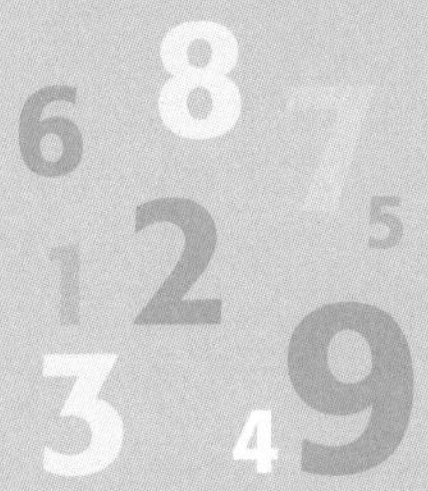

**What to look for:** These children absolutely adore anything to do with code cracking in the full sense of the term. They just love cracking riddles, crosswords, world mysteries in ANY field: jigsaws, maths and science problems, even the dishwasher if it blows up. Typically, code crackers are natural sleuths. Mysteries are their ultimate playing field, whether that is figuring out what happened to the neighbour's cat, where the goldfish really went and who was responsible, as well as where you last left your car keys when you got in from getting the groceries. Don't try hiding treats – the code cracker will find them.

**Delving deeper:** New young teachers are often on alert when code crackers are around because they seem to have an innate ability to figure out who is dating who in the staff room. Code crackers like anything that gives their brilliant brain a challenge.

**In the future:** Code crackers make natural and brilliant troubleshooters in any field they choose; be that working as an investigative journalist for *The New York Times*, solving a great mystery of archaeology or figuring out how to cure cancer.

## The enquirer

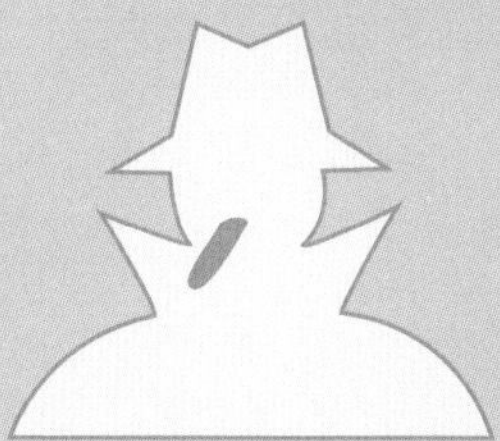

**What to look for:** A natural magpie, an enquirer's bedroom is like the original 'old curiosity shop' full of all sorts of things spanning topics from sea life to space. Mention something in a wide range of subject areas and the chances are enquirers know something about it. They enjoy adult conversation as much as peer conversation because, well, for enquirers it depends on who can tell them the most about something at any given time. You see, curiosity is everything to enquirers, it is what courses through their veins day and night and makes them jump out of bed in the morning. As a consequence, they are not afraid to ask the 'Big Questions' while you are at the checkout counter, last thing on a Friday night: 'Mum, where do I come from? How big do you think the universe really is? Do you think there is a way we could clean up the planet?'

**Delving deeper:** These children need meaty challenges in any field they encounter to really engage their curious minds and bring out their brilliance. They bring the same tenacity to answer questions to even such 'vitally important' ideas as 'Why I should have a new pair of trainers'. Teachers think twice when negotiating topics with enquirers as they will have explored all arguments first and be ready with perfectly solid answers at every turn.

**In the future:** Enquirers are drawn to any topic that allows them to feel there is a lot to find out, and perhaps with a never-ending journey ahead. NASA might be a perfect destination for them to use their gifts, as would be any field that allows them to keep on asking those big questions.

## The visionary

**What to look for:** Think Da Vinci and Howard Hughes and you are on the right track. Basically, visionary children are highly imaginative and creative people who are able to visualize new ideas: a flying car, the next method of transport, houses of the future. Indeed, they are capable of changing the way you think and live, regularly challenging you to 'think outside the box'.

**Delving deeper:** Visionaries can drive you mad because they tend to work on an idea almost obsessively, day and night. Sleep may mean very little to them at such times, as might also food. A visionary is not particularly mindful of convention, preferring to stand out from the crowd. They can do this without even trying, which is why you might get a few letters home from school. Doodles are sometimes preferable to doing more mundane or repetitive tasks in class.

**In the future:** Visionaries can excel in any field where their abilities are respected and valued: fashion design, architecture, engineering, music, film making. You name it, their visionary capabilities will put them in good stead.

## The constructor

**What to look for:** As soon as constructors climb out of nappies, they find a way to build something that helps them climb out of their cradles. If you leave anything around, a constructor finds it and builds something out of it. They simply can't resist any toy or game that involves … yes, you said it, building and creating something. They see in multi-dimensions so they have an uncanny ability to see exactly how something may or may not be able to fit together. When they get older, constructors will be able to reverse a wide car into a narrow garage, no problem, as their spatial ability is that good. Taking the recent robotic toy or new bicycle apart is a very attractive option for the constructor. I mean, why ride a bike when you can figure out how it is built and may be able to design one of your own?

**Delving deeper:** Sitting still and doing nothing is not an option for the constructor. Basically, they are fidgets. Walking and moving is like part of their life support system. If they sit still, they feel a bit like a sea creature that has to keep moving to breathe! Building and doing is great, sitting and doing nothing isn't.

**In the future:** Such children are good at anything that allows them to get to the heart of how anything works and is constructed. They will succeed in any field, from building rockets to designing a new computer. Whatever it is, they will build it and build it well. Oh, and if you were ever to get stuck at the top of Mount Everest – the constructor is the best person to figure out a way down.

## The fairy tale teller

**What to look for:** Imagination and creative thinking is wild. The fairy tale teller can be a quiet, read-and-write-in-a-corner person or a loud, chat-and-write-in-a-corner person. Either way, these children's creations have you entranced as one minute their brains are in Disney and they are Pocahontas or the next they are in Jurassic Park chasing dinosaurs, and you are invited to join in, as long as you stick to their story line. Fairy tale tellers use any and all mediums to make their imaginative creations come to life, including the written word, art, collections of objects, computer imagery. Never get between such children and their work as when they are in the middle of a story, they like to finish it to absolute perfection (which may take weeks), and no – you can't help!

**Delving deeper:** Dreaminess can be misconstrued as vagueness. There is nothing vague about the storyteller; dreaminess is just part of the process of freeing up creativity and imagination. They can often miss over the detail of grammar and spelling in favour of getting a great idea across.

**In the future:** Always listen to fairy tale tellers when they have gone through the trouble of writing a special story or poem for you. They will otherwise hold it against you for hours, no, make that years. So listen up and look suitably impressed – this could be the next J.K. Rowling.

## The abstract thinker

**What to look for:** Abstract thinkers enjoy considering things in a way that doesn't ordinarily strike you when you look at things. They can be very good at non-verbal puzzles or tests that don't rely on numbers or letters, but on making sense of things in visual terms. Look at a painting and the abstract thinker will be able to point out things you may not have considered, unless perhaps you had been trained: the way the artist constructed the painting, how the shadow and light fall and what effect this has on the way the picture is laid out. Such children can sometimes find putting thoughts into words less than easy because what they are thinking is, well, 'abstract' and so moves beyond just words. They can quite often be easy as a child, because they can be quite happy to quietly get on with something they enjoy and that interests them without needing that much supervision.

**Delving deeper:** Abstract thinkers can sometimes amaze their teachers with their observations, or with what catches their fancy. They are very quick at pointing things out and making you see something that may have missed your attention when you looked at it the first time around. They can apply this gift to any field across science, art, mathematics, bringing their original ways to looking at things. They particularly enjoy open-ended questions in homework where they can research interesting facts and not feel limited to think in just one way about what they are doing.

**In the future:** Abstract thinking is not limited to any one field and has applications in areas as diverse as architecture, choreography and science.

## The great entertainer

**What to look for:** Roll up, roll up! Whether it is their ability to write songs from an early age, or captivate an audience with their acting, singing or dancing ability (or combinations of these), or simply bowl people over with their personality and highly developed sense of humour – just standing there, they have presence and entertain. Such children are dangerous when it comes to getting their own way, though: to sway the argument, they can turn on 'dog eyes' just at the strategic point.

**Delving deeper:** Entertainers' skills are great when they write their first play in junior school, but less so when they decide to entertain their class with brilliant jokes they heard last week and their teacher is trying to keep the classroom quiet. Entertainers can have tremendous empathy, too, so that when it comes to casting who should be who in the school play this year, they know exactly who should have which part and why. Great entertainers are rarely short of friends – everyone loves them.

**In the future:** Wherever they work, whatever they do, they will be stars because their personality, energy and ability make them stand out. They are most obviously likely to succeed in the film and music industries; but less obviously can make extraordinarily good scientists who are able to make science accessible and understandable to many people. Students at college might yearn for a professor like this. No day will ever be boring with the great entertainer around.

## The turbo-chatterbox

**What to look for:** This is the child who sits next to you on a plane travelling from New York to Delhi – and doesn't stop talking all the way. Such children are a) not at all verbally challenged and b) have a really bright mind. And you know what makes someone like this hold your attention all the way from New York to Delhi? They are amazing and great company. Never get into an argument with a turbo-chatterbox, not only will they always have the last word, they will always out argue and outwit you, too. You see, to talk that fast, all of the time, anywhere, any time, you have to be able to think fast too. A turbo-chatterbox can even out talk you when eating.

**Delving deeper:** Such children are naturally gifted verbal communicators and will bring that passion and ability to any language – including maths. Communicating ideas fast in any sector for any field verbally is what they are into. And as long as they can do that, they are happy to work anywhere – except in classrooms or offices where they might have to keep quiet for too long – now that is hard work.

**In the future:** Turbo-chatterboxes are people who are going to grow up to do well in areas like law where the people they represent will love them for their quick thinking mind and high command of an extremely sophisticated vocabulary.

## The little old man or woman

**What to look for:** Little old men or women appear to have an innate wisdom older than their actual years. And the annoying thing for adults is that most of the time their comments are actually right. A little old woman isn't trying to be older than her years; it's just that adults aren't seeing her for what she actually is: a little person. And a little old man isn't only a little person, he has a really strong gift of that often forgotten but widely cherished thing called common sense. This gift is the most underrated of all in today's times. A person can have great gifts, but not the common sense to put on a jacket when going out in the snow – that'd be the visionary we discussed earlier, who would rush out without a care for a coat while they were focusing on their next big idea. The little old man or woman would shake their head at this kind of lack of common sense, pointing out that not wearing a coat in the cold was a recipe for getting ill. And they would be right, of course!

**Delving deeper:** Little old women or men will often put their teachers, parents and elder siblings to rights with some good old-fashioned rational thinking. In effect, they are natural born philosophers with something sensible and well thought through to say about everything and anything. You see, for these children, they have a gravitas, even at such a young age, and understand that whatever happens, it is all in 'life's rich tapestry'.

**In the future:** Future careers can include being on think tanks to sort out world problems, writing a book called 'common sense' – whoops, can't do that as it has already been written by another great philosopher – but you get my drift. They will be sorting out other people at work in either a management or counselling role: much-loved future leaders.

## The young tycoon

**What to look for:** At the age of five, the young tycoon has a garage sale and makes a tidy profit from the proceeds. When starting school, there is a way to turn sweets into a bank. At secondary school, there is enough time to grow lettuce and do homework; then by selling the lettuce, there is money to spare for more seeds to grow next year, and flowers too. These are a big hit with the chums at school, who buy bunch loads.

**Delving deeper:** The young tycoon gets a job during the summer school holidays and saves all the capital to raise funds for the next 'project'. At school, the child perseveres, but is often bored and decides to take a year out before going to university … the rest is history.

**In the future:** Young tycoons make a million before they are 20. They are natural born entrepreneurs with a flair for seeking out a gap in the market and giving that market exactly the product it needs, at exactly the right time, in order to make another great business success.

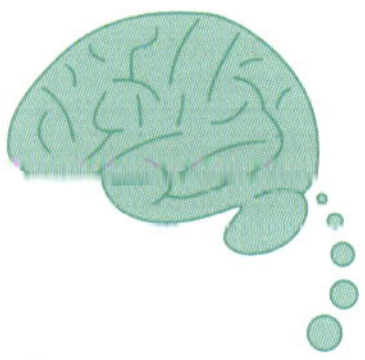

**Brilliant fact!**

Having a condition such as Asperger's or dyslexia does not preclude any child or person from having outstanding ability in any given field.

## STEP 4

### Think about your child's personal interests

Gifts and abilities can also reside in things that children do outside school. So now is the time to think fully about and make a note of all the interests your child enjoys and/or excels at outside school. This could be cookery, a sport of some kind: soccer; skateboarding; horse riding; ice hockey. It could be a musical or dance interest, or even volunteer work, which indicates they like working with people and making others feel valued. All of these things are important in the search for a child's range of gifts and abilities.

## STEP 5

### Bring it all together

As you bring together all the information you have collected in these steps, remember that there is no ready-made description for the unique combination of abilities that your child possesses.

Now is the time to take stock of what you have discovered together. Look back over the pages in your notebook, taking information from each step to form a summary of all your child's gifts and abilities. Use the checklist below to help you remember to include everything you have discovered. Your child is about to turn an important corner in their life, having reached the moment of a powerful self-realization: your child is beginning to understand how many gifts and abilities they possess. Every child is brilliant, period.

If your child had any doubts about this, then those doubts should now be gone, giving way to a huge door of opportunity opening up to them. Rich in the knowledge they now have about their individual gifts and abilities, your child can look forward to their future, confident in their own brilliance. This is their time.

## STEP 6

### The most important step of all; value and believe in your own individual gifts

We live in an age where media images massively influence how we think about ourselves and each other. It is not unusual, therefore, for today's children to be so captivated by the gifts of others they see on TV, that they don't always appreciate and value their own gifts.

## **Considering your notes** checklist

✓ Which gifts and abilities stand out?

✓ Can you and your child think of anything you haven't covered already?

✓ What does your child think are their main strengths and gifts?

✓ Are there any areas that you have discussed that your child can now move forward in more confidently?

✓ If the answer to the last question is uncertain, then follow through and get the problem sorted out sooner rather than later.

✓ Now ask your child to sum up all of their special gifts in one or two sentences.

# Discovering gifts in children with dyslexia and Asperger's

When I first began working in the field of gifted children I worked with children with different conditions including Asperger's and dyslexia. Asperger's is the higher functioning aspect of autistic spectrum disorder or ASD. Children with Asperger's can often have savant-like qualities; namely they will have an islet of ability that may be extraordinary in, for example, music, art or mathematics. Often children with Asperger's, because of the qualities of their condition, can find it difficult to be around others in close proximity. But this shouldn't preclude such children from having the choice to be a part of wider activities, such as summer camps, which can enable their horizons to be broadened just like any other child. Furthermore, the results can be tremendous not just for the children themselves but also for educating their peers that having Asperger's does not preclude them from having special gifts, indeed their gifts can be amazing.

Dyslexia is not just one condition but can display itself in many forms. But what is clear from the research to date is that children with dyslexia are much more likely to be highly visual thinkers than their peers and this has real benefits in terms of thinking speed. Seeing in pictures as opposed to words, for example, can make children with dyslexia think much more quickly in certain situations.

It is for this reason that people with dyslexia often make good mountaineers, racing drivers and business people, all areas where thinking fast and on their feet is particularly important. If you are not convinced, just take a look at the facts. Richard Branson, the founder of the massive company Virgin, is dyslexic, as is the highly successful actor Tom Cruise. People with dyslexia can also make extremely good artists and architects – in other words, having dyslexia equals having special gifts and a brilliant brain. The key to making sure any child with dyslexia succeeds is having it spotted early on so that teachers are aware and everyone can work positively in the same direction – and that is, of course, upwards and onwards.

If you or someone in your family is interested in reading more about dual ability in children, namely the fact that having Asperger's or dyslexia does not mean that they are not also blessed with having brilliant gifts and talents, then please see Further reading on page 154.

Children are naturally creatures of survival, programmed to seek out routes to successful, happy and prosperous lifestyles. In a world where children are constantly presented with images of certain gifts and abilities appearing to lead to glamorous lifestyles on TV, it is hardly surprising that when you ask them what they want to be when they grow up, a great many reply with the stock answers: sports star, celebrity, actress, singer, dancer. I am not suggesting for one minute that all of these things are not brilliant in their own right, but the point for children to remember is that gifts come in all kinds of packages. And one of the major steps in children realizing the brilliant opportunities afforded by their own gifts is to value and believe in them.

This is the foundation upon which a child can make their own dreams come to fruition. If at any time your child has any self-doubt, share with them the mantra created opposite, and your child will be on the route to success again.

## STEP 7

**Look for new opportunities because with them come new possibilities**

During my work with parents, children and schools, I often find out a lot about the children when I take them out of their school and home environments and see how they fare when presented with new or different challenges. These challenges open up different ways of thinking for children as they are often presented with opportunities to find out more about their range of gifts and abilities and how their brain works.

Often children surprise themselves in these challenges by finding out that they have hidden abilities they didn't know they had until then. The child who is quiet at school and doesn't often take the lead might discover untold leadership qualities by organizing their mates in an outward-bound challenge up in the mountains. A child who is afraid to share their ideas in class, suddenly finds they have a fantastic ability when it comes to solving abstract problems involving numbers, letters or shapes.

The point is this: children are developing every day and so are their brains. With new challenges come new opportunities and discoveries about their range of gifts and talents – so be prepared to continue to be amazed at what you both might find with each new challenge that life presents!

## A child's mantra for success: I value my gifts!

Congratulations to me!

I am special
I am unique
I value my gifts
I believe in me

I hereby declare that I am brilliant!
Hurrah for me!

Signed ____________________

Date ____________________

I AM BRILLIANT

# The **route** to **success** 2

Well done! Now that you have reached the end of this chapter you and your child are both fully aware of the range of gifts and different abilities that your child possesses. You've learned a lot in the process, and here is a recap of the key points.

1 **Brilliance begins in ordinary homes with ordinary families.** Brilliance starts with parents knowing what to look for and how to develop the natural gifts in their child. Brilliance isn't all in the genes; it is about children having their gifts spotted, understood and supported at the right time so they don't miss out on vital opportunities.

Read the story of Lenny on page 36 and the five truths of brilliance on pages 37–9 to find out what how brilliance really gets started.

2 **When thinking about your child's gifts, think clusters not pigeonholes.** Gifts and abilities overlap and work together within the individual child. Think of your child's gifts and abilities as like the rings that ripple outward from a rock in a lake. Start from your child's unique person and work out from there.

Read the case studies of David Beckham and Donald Trump on page 38 to remind your child that the roots of brilliance lie in learning how to make their gifts work for them.

3 **Low boredom thresholds can give rise to mischievousness in the classroom, but can also be a strong sign of brilliance.** If your child is complaining of boredom a little too frequently, take it seriously and act now. Once teachers are aware they will be only too happy to help you out.

Work through 'Discovering your child's hidden gifts: Part I' with your child on pages 44–7 to ascertain what needs to be done next.

4 **Not all gifts are obvious.** When Einstein said that, 'Not everything that can be counted counts and not everything that counts can be counted', he was talking about the limits of mathematics to fully understand the universe. The same may be said of the limits tests have to capture children's abilities.

Visit 'Discovering your child's hidden gifts Part I: Mistaken identities' and 'Part II: Reading all the signs' on pages 44–53.

5 **Children's gifts can be masked by labels being attached to them too early.** The 'bossy boots' may not be bossy but, in fact, a great leader and facilitator. Similarly, the child who turns their pocket money into a bank is just exploring their natural entrepreneurial ability, they may be a 'young tycoon'.

Read 'Discovering your child's hidden gifts Part II: Reading all the signs' on pages 47–53. Make a note of anything that, now you are aware of what to look for, rings true for your own child.

6 **Children with special educational needs can also have brilliant gifts and abilities in many different areas.**

Read page 55 and Further reading on page 154 to get more information about why understanding this is vital to all children being able to realize their individual gifts.

7 **Children need to believe in and value their own special gifts and abilities.** Children are bombarded with media images of people with certain gifts that seem to be successful. This can lead children to want to be like someone else, instead of valuing and celebrating their own individual gifts.

To help your child celebrate who they are and what their special gifts are, let them copy or make their own version of 'A child's mantra for success: I value my gifts!' on page 57.

# 3

One rainy Sunday afternoon I was watching an old black and white 1940s' movie on TV. It was a product of that era when custard pie comedy was very much the fashion. At one point, the kind hero is making a house call on a friend, except that he has made a mistake; the door he is about to open is not his friend's but that of another house. Inside, a massive custard pie fight has erupted. The pies are flying everywhere. As our innocent hero opens the door, smack! He gets hit in quick succession with about eight custard pies. Not deserving this, our hero stands there feeling a tad confused.

In my seminars there are no custard pies, but there are a lot of confused parents. They are confused because they have been hit with a succession of buzz words when it comes to answering the question, 'How does my child learn best?' There are many ways of learning out there and it is hard to make head or tail of them when you don't really know what they are. This chapter helps you find out what all the fuss is about so you are better informed about which opportunities might benefit your child.

When looking to answer the question of how your child is best able to learn, don't start with theories, start with your child. Theories are fine, but there is just one problem with them – not all the theories fit all of the children all of the time because of one very simple scientific fact: everyone is different. We need to celebrate that and make that the starting point. So take from theories what works for your child, rather than trying to make the theory fit the child. Sure, we all share some basic brain physiology, but in approaching how your child learns best, take your lead from medical science, which has found the 'one size fits all' theory is defunct and definitely not the way of the future.

The next era of medicine will be more effective than in past generations because it is tailor made to your precise biochemistry. Reflect this in your approach: your child doesn't need 'one size fits all' theories, instead use the knowledge outlined overleaf to help your child become totally confident in their learning. Your child can tailor-make a system of learning that works for them, which is the purpose of this chapter. It:

★ gives you and your child the knowledge you need to understand and evaluate for yourselves buzz words and different theories about learning.

★ provides your child with the opportunity to experiment with several different techniques so that they can find out what works best for them.

★ explains the foundations of personalized learning for children.

# Different ways of **learning**

## BUZZ WORD 1: VAK

VAK is certainly not new but remains a constant buzz word in learning, wherever you are in the world. VAK stands for: visual, auditory and kinaesthetic. The idea behind it is that we are all either mainly a visual, auditory or kinaesthetic learner.

★ Visual learners need to see things before they can really learn them best.

★ Auditory learners learn best when they listen to someone explain something.

★ Kinaesthetic learners are hands-on learners. This means that they if they have the chance to actually do something, they are more likely to learn it.

Of course, it stands to reason that if we are born able to see, listen and feel, then we cannot be just learning using one sense. In reality, every day we take information from our environment using all our senses. But at the same time, there is evidence to suggest that people are more likely to have a preference for learning that is geared to one of these three. I have seen instances where children are indeed attracted to visual rather than, say, auditory learning, but at other times I have found children who enjoy a good mixture, combining all three.

A lot depends on the child, but it also depends upon what the child is learning. For example, when learning languages, some children just need to hear a word in order to remember it, whereas others feel much better if they see it written down. But just looking at a car isn't going to mean that you can then immediately know how to drive it – in that instance, kinaesthetic learning is going to be important.

State-of-the-art thinking and research in neuroscience suggests that the best learning engages seeing, hearing and touching at the same time.

★ Each type of learning enables the brain to store and retrieve information on a number of different levels. In real terms, this is like the layering in a coffee cake; the richer the layers, the more embedded the learning is within the brain.

★ To open up new pathways of learning, let your child find ways of understanding new topics using visual, auditory *and* kinaesthetic techniques or using them in surprising and different ways.

Experiment now with VAK in the exercise 'When is an apple ever an apple?', opposite.

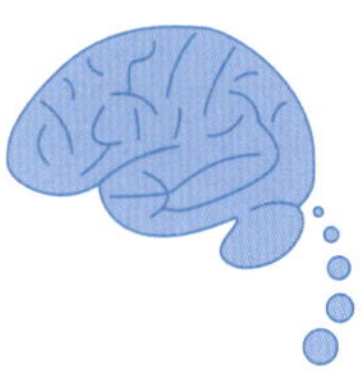

### Brilliant fact!

The VAK theory can be as restricting as it is liberating. For example, children can shut down the possibility of learning by doing, because they have been told that they are 'visual learners'. This is a distortion of what VAK is really about and is not useful, because if we were born only to learn in one way like that, we would not have the full range of senses at our disposal. When children are reminded of this, they can successfully keep their options open and not set false limits on themselves.

*Robert wanted to do better in his French homework. But he found that he had a real problem learning new words. I observed with his parents how he was learning. His habit was to try to sit quietly and remember the new information by repeating it out loud. This worked but he found it wound him up and after a number of weeks it had begun to backfire. The more he tried to do this, the more wound-up he became. Robert was on a downward spiral. His brain was like a wheel stuck in a muddy ditch. It was just spinning around and needed something to break the cycle. If not, Robert might be switched off from language learning forever.*

*To find a way to trick his brain into thinking about learning language in a different way, I found out from his parents what he liked doing by way of relaxation. Robert really enjoyed swimming, so I suggested to him that for just one session he should try a novel approach to language learning. I picked out some vocabulary to learn and as he swam, he repeated the words gently in his head, each time alternating his stroke to match a new word or pattern in a verb he was learning.*

*The result was amazing. Robert found that because he was already relaxed, the learning came faster. Also, the rhythm of the swimming regulated the rhythm of the words he was learning, so he didn't get frustrated. There was no magic to the success of this learning activity. In real terms, this activity had opened up a new way for Robert's mind to learn and internalize this information and, at the same time, it broke a negative association in his mind about language learning, introducing a more positive one. Anyone can do this, not just Robert.*

# When is an apple ever an apple?

Take the concept 'apple' and see how far you would get if you could only teach someone what an apple is using one of the following methods:

**Visual**
You can't use words and you can't use the actual object, you just have to explain to that person what an apple is using a drawing.

**Auditory**
The person cannot see and nor can they touch the object. You can only explain to them what an apple is by giving a verbal description.

**Kinaesthetic**
The person can neither see nor hear, they can only feel the apple to be able to understand what it is.

When you and your child have finished the exercise together, discuss the following questions:

**1** How easy was it for either of you to explain the concept 'apple' using only visual, auditory or kinaesthetic techniques?

**2** If you had never come across the concept 'apple' before, how would you each prefer to learn about it – using just one method or using a combination?

Remember that there are no right or wrong answers here, just a conversation about how you feel about VAK to evaluate this theory for yourself.

# What's in a brain wave?

If you have ever wondered what brain activity looks like when you or your child are doing different activities, then you need wonder no more, here they are, from alpha to delta brain wave patterns.

**Alpha brain waves**
The 'daydream' state when your child's imagination runs riot.

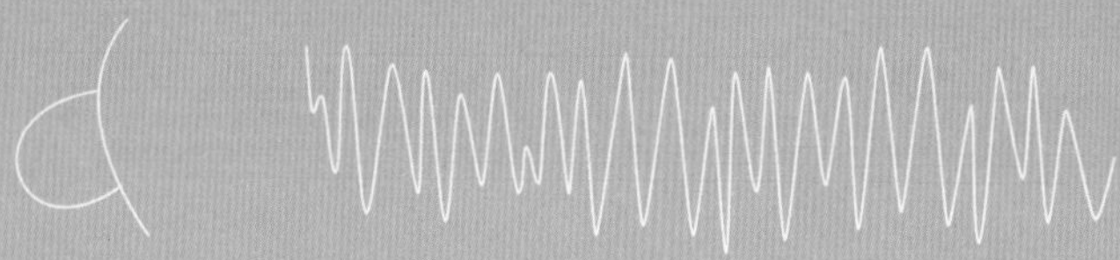

**Beta brain waves**
A logical thought pattern when your child is speaking or doing something.

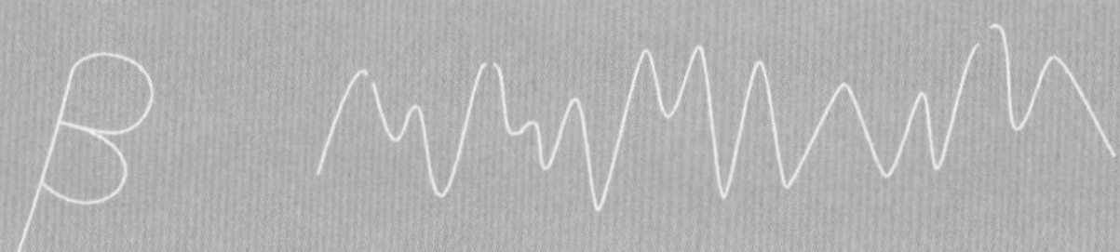

**Theta brain waves**
Inspiration and creativity at work! Your child must not be disturbed at this point – creativity is peaking!

**Delta brain waves**
Your child is asleep but not dreaming!

## BUZZ WORD 2: BRAIN MUSIC

Research has found that when people play Mozart before taking an intelligence test their score has increased. This information has been around for over a decade now. A lot of the fuss arose because it has long been known that Albert Einstein would take up his violin and play Mozart whenever he found he had a mental block – and the process seemed to work as he found he could then continue working successfully. But whether that had more to do with the nature of Mozart's music or just the act of playing music, which can enhance left-right brain connectivity, or whether it might also have been the physiology of him getting up and playing the violin, or a combination of all these factors is not, of course, known.

What seems to have been less popularized in the media, however, is the fact that different kinds of music seem to induce different brain states. The most established example is the Baroque music of Bach, Albinoni and Handel, which can produce a relaxed, yet alert mental state in the brain that is particularly good for helping both adults and children learn. From neuroscience we can see the brain in different states of rest, alertness and so on, as shown in the illustration 'What's in a brain wave?', left.

On the other hand, research has found that rock music has sparked violent behaviour in laboratory rats in cages. The reasons behind these startling findings are not yet fully understood, but let's just say that until further research emerges, I prefer not to use much rock music in my seminars with children! Baroque music, however, is a different matter. It's the kind of music that once you have it on in the background, you never know it's there and I have found that it does indeed help adults and children to focus when they need to concentrate. The effect that Baroque music has on the brain appears to be rooted in the facts that:

★ Its rhythm and constancy work particularly harmoniously with the brain's own natural brain wave rhythms.

★ It encourages the brain's natural preference for left-right brain connectivity.

*Elena was having trouble whenever she had to stand up in front of her class and give a presentation. She had had one experience that didn't go well and this had meant that whenever it came to making a presentation, nerves got the better of her. She had lost her confidence. First I wanted her to think of the concept 'presentation' as not just one thing: standing up and talking, but for her to know that she did indeed have the natural ability to make a presentation in front of her classmates. I knew, for example, that she was extremely confident in dance and regularly performed in front of her peers. Yet she didn't link the confidence she had in dance with the other kind of performance: presentations in front of her class.*

*The key, then, was to translate Elena's confidence in physical performance into verbal performance. So I devised a dance in which she had to mix words, symbols and movement to tell a story. I set the dance to Baroque music to set up a mental trigger so that whenever she heard the same music she would remember her successful experience in the exercise. When she was preparing for her presentation she could also switch on the music to help her regain that relaxed yet alert state.*

*The transition was successful. The result was that Elena was able to stand up with confidence and to deliver her presentations in class, and she was thrilled. Anyone can do this. There is no magic or trickery, it is just taking basic facts from neuroscience and applying them to how we approach problems like this in learning.*

## BUZZ WORD 3: ACCELERATION

If you just think about the volume and speed with which new information, facts and knowledge reach your child on an hour-to-hour or even minute-to-minute basis, life moves fast today. This is in no small part due to an explosion in technology. Now cast yourself back to when you were the same age and it was most probably just a TV and stereo that you had to listen to.

Now think about how children feel when they go to school and have to wait for someone to explain a new topic. I am not having a 'go' at teachers (most of the ones I meet are working very hard), just pointing out that children are used to pressing a button and – boom! – they have instant information in full colour on a wide screen; an all-singing, all-dancing experience.

Classrooms are adapting – depending on their funds, some faster or slower than others – but, nevertheless, our children can be forgiven for feeling impatient, even bored sometimes, because they want to move on quicker, faster, better. Their era is all about speed. When it comes to information, they don't know how to wait, and should they have to? This presents the greatest challenge for education today everywhere, bar developing countries where the technology boom has not yet taken off.

Now then, you might be wondering why I have given you all that information. Well, if you find your child is regularly bored at school; chews up school work at a rate of knots; appears to need challenge as the rule

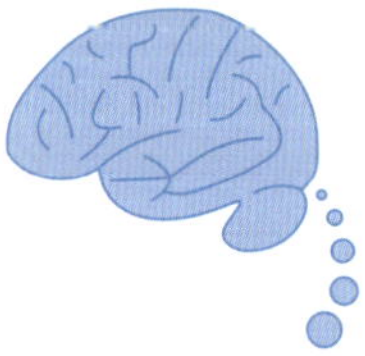

**Brilliant fact!**
Support, encourage but never push children. Pushing backfires. Support and encouragement always wins the day and delivers success – for them and for you.

rather than the exception, and finds what they are doing in the next class up is more interesting … it is time to think about acceleration.

Age and ability are not interdependent. If children want to move on and feel confident in doing so, they should be allowed to have that choice. Acceleration is more established in some countries than others, but, basically, wherever you are, it means skipping a class to enable a child to move at a more suitable pace.

Acceleration remains controversial, despite it having been around for some time. So before going this route, check out all the options besides acceleration first. Remember that there are always at least two ways to achieve or do anything. Look at all the options, discuss it with your child fully, and then inform your choice by working with and listening to those teachers that work with your child on a daily basis; an informed decision is always the best decision. Of paramount importance, you must make sure your child is fully in on the decision and is happy with the idea.

## BUZZ WORD 4: ENRICHMENT

Enrichment programmes come in a variety of forms, all of which are aimed at the same thing: providing depth and width to what children are already learning at school. Examples of enrichment could be:

★ After-school special interest groups, such as dance, art, maths, drama or science.

★ Attending a summer school.

★ Attending extra clubs or sessions on particular areas of the curriculum.

All of these are great for children, not only in academic terms but also for developing wider interest and friendship groups. However, when it comes to enrichment programmes, as with acceleration, what may sound a good idea to you, may not sound as good to your child.

Being packed off to summer school is not the same thing as having had the opportunity to choose it yourself. Many a cartoon figure from Charlie Brown to Bart Simpson has rued the day they have to go to summer camp. It can be the stuff of dreams or nightmares, depending on which camp they go to.

Children are tough negotiators – just like you! So do your homework first: let your child do the sleuthing with you and find out about any enrichment programmes on offer. Then when you have amassed all the facts together, jot down the advantages and disadvantages of the different options in your notebook.

When you have discussed the pros and cons, make a decision together and you have a good deal. You both win.

## **Acceleration** checklist

✓ Check that adjustments could be made within your child's class to better deal with their ability and provide more opportunity for challenge.

✓ Then discuss with your child what might be the best way forward – stay put or move up.

✓ Discuss all of this with your child's teachers.

✓ Think about the consequences in full: areas like friendship groups could be affected if your child moves up too quickly.

✓ The upside is that your child may not feel bored any more.

✓ The downside is that your child might be lonely.

✓ Don't act in haste; instead – think, reflect and then make the decision together.

✓ Remember – happiness first and then you'll find the learning follows naturally.

## BUZZ WORD 5: TARGET SETTING

Target setting is all about, well, target setting! If it is done well in school, it is a process whereby the teacher and the child sit down together, have a chat about how to progress in different areas, and then together set some realistic targets for the coming weeks. In reality, with masses to get through in the daily routine and curriculum in school, it means that this can be a more or less thorough process depending on time available.

More valuable for children is to learn how to set targets for themselves, as opposed to seeing targets as something someone else sets for them. This may seem a subtle point, but as you will come to see in Chapter 7, it is a crucial step in a child's route to success. Learning to set realistic targets is a part of children becoming more confident in learning. By thinking about and setting themselves targets, children become self-motivated and more self-directed learners, set for a cycle of positive life-long learning. To get your child into the habit of target setting now, follow the checklist, below right.

When children have judged whether or not they have met their targets, they can reward themselves with a star or other symbol stuck onto a special place. Stickers like this cost peanuts, but the cycle the process sets up in a child's mind is priceless.

The art of self-rewarding is not about the price of the object, it is about the actual act itself. It sets up a healthy can-do cycle in a child's mind that says, 'I don't need someone else to reward me, I reward myself'. And at a deeper brain level this is setting up a very important message: self-confidence and self-belief. It's like learning how to swim without the water wings on. They can do it on their own.

## BUZZ WORD 6: PERSONALIZED LEARNING

Personalized learning means exactly what it says: realizing that learning is personal and that no two children will learn best in precisely the same way. This has always been my philosophy and now thankfully many a government project is moving this way; I see this as both logical and great news for our children. At the same time, it is not easy for teachers to deliver personalized learning in practice in a busy classroom. This is because many classrooms were not originally designed with personalized learning as the focus; traditionally classrooms were built, of course, to deliver a curriculum to all children in the same way.

Personalized learning is important not only for children, but for adults. It enables you both to know how you learn best and to benefit from whatever you are trying to learn. You and your child can learn to do this at home with this chapter. Following the steps on personalized learning on pages 68–75 will enable your child to find out how they learn best and thus benefit in all areas of their school work, including homework, revision and class work. Knowing what works best for them means that children can then get the best out of school.

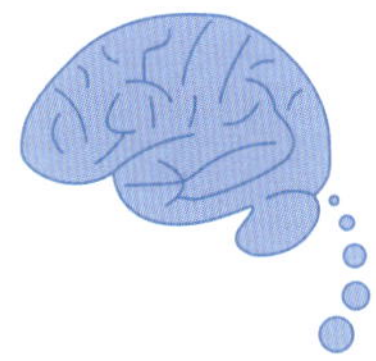

**Brilliant fact!**

If you are forever the one setting targets for your child and the reward is food or other gifts, not only does it get expensive, your child is doing it for you rather than themselves. In the long run, that isn't the best way to go and builds up tensions that don't need to be there.

## **Target setting** checklist

✓ Sit down and chat about progress with your child in different areas. Make the tone gentle.

✓ It is crucial that you let your child set the target, not you. To begin with, it could be something as simple as, 'Set my homework out better'. Start small and grow from there.

✓ Have another chat at the end of the week, asking how well your child has got on with the target(s) – and encourage honesty! Let your child be the judge.

# The **seven steps** to personalized **learning**

Einstein is alleged to have said that the biggest enemy of progress is authority. What you have been taught about learning for years is just that: what you have been taught; it doesn't necessarily make it accurate or right. Remember that for centuries the world was flat until all hell was let loose when someone found out that it was, in fact, round! To really begin to tailor-make a system of learning that works for you, is a bit like bungee jumping. You have to forget what you have been taught about gravity and dive in. And when you do, you will be so glad you did it, because learning will be a joy and you will find you can learn just about anything. The steps that start to the right and run on to page 75 work just as well for you and your child – enjoy! You need never be stumped again.

Each of the seven steps towards personalized learning are summarized for you in the 'Pyramid to tailor-made personalized learning', opposite. Everything you and your child ever need to know about how to personalize your learning, by enabling you to figure out a system that works for you, is contained within the pyramid. So let's get underway with finding out how your child can benefit by understanding a few basic concepts and techniques of personalized learning.

## STEP 1

**Never be passive, always be active**

Cultivate a healthy irreverence for the way information is arranged in textbooks and presented to you. Don't allow yourself to get into the habit of passively accepting that when you are presented with text, the way things are set out in it is necessarily the best way for YOU to learn. If it doesn't work for you, don't hesitate. Take action! Jot down notes first from the text and then have a good old time mixing it up and changing it around. Do it your way.

To test drive this in practice, and for your child to learn how powerful a learning tool this approach is, take a look at 'Cultivating active learning', overleaf.

## STEP 2

**Learn how to make knowledge your own**

Humans love what they own. To be really effective learners, children need to feel full ownership of a topic by personalizing it so that possession of that knowledge is complete – that is how the brain works. Whenever they are given a new topic to learn, children need to know one thing: go wild and be creative. Make a rhyme about it; make a dance about it; do both.

The activity 'Bringing creativity into learning', overleaf, shows just how creative you and your child can be. But don't stop there, take another topic, maybe something that your child is doing at school or is interested in outside school, and have a go at making another mobile; making another dance and rhyme; making up a play or a song. Why not? It is fun.

Each time children do something like this, their mind is linking learning with fun – and that is great motivation for a child to learn and do more. By making something of their own – a mobile, for example – children are better able to remember the facts about the topic.

## STEP 3

**Experiment with different techniques**

The key to finding what works for your child in terms of learning techniques, is to experiment. You and your child have already learned about different ways of thinking and learning, which at each turn opens up new opportunities for how your child learns best.

But when it comes to personalized learning, it is only by experimenting with new ideas that you find out what works best. What is certain is that once your child's brain has this new knowledge, it will

## Pyramid to tailor-made personal learning

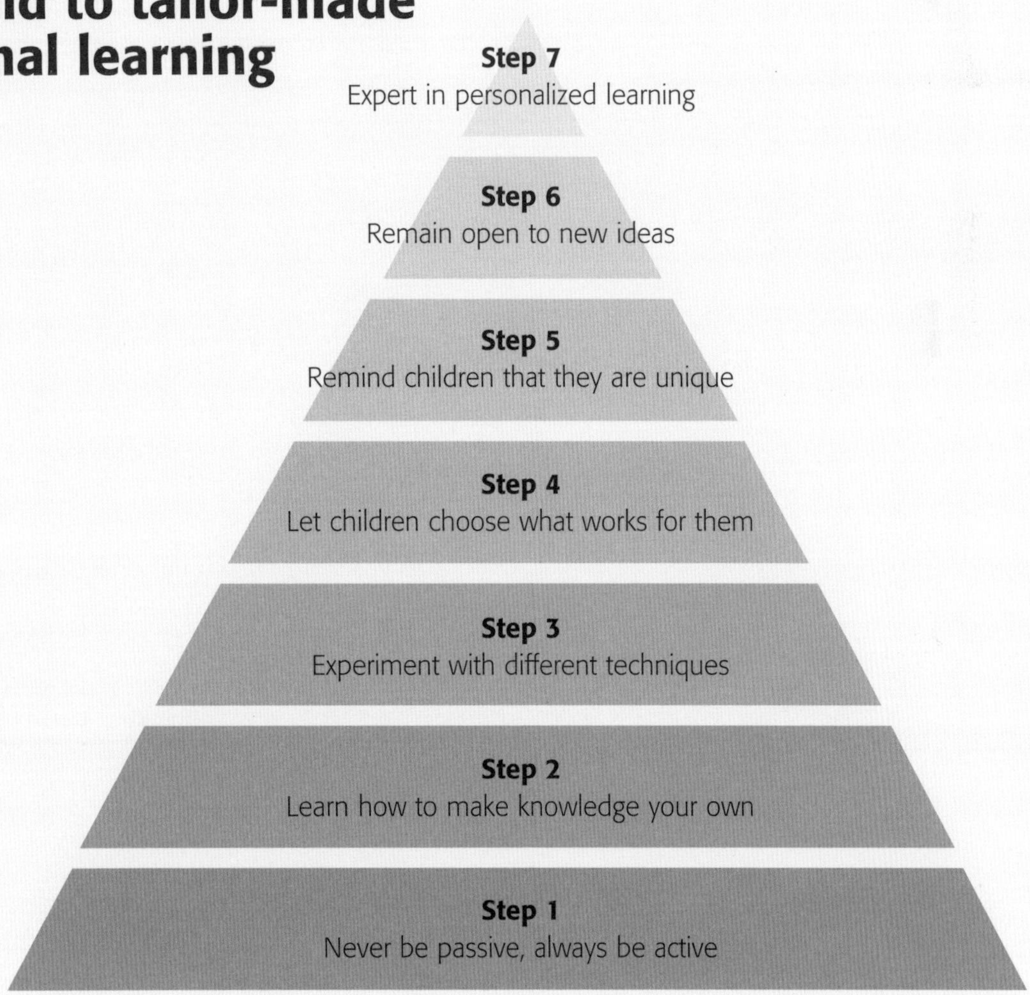

# Cultivating active learning

The text below on *Ursus maritimus* shows how you might normally be presented with facts in a standard textbook. Below this, I have rearranged all the information to suit how I want to learn and remember the facts. Try this yourself, by looking up facts about another animal or mammal; it could be a dolphin, tiger or armadillo. The minute you start rearranging the text you are beginning to take charge of the information so that it works for you, not the person who wrote it. And that is the beginning of personalizing your learning. No matter what the topic

**You will need:** paper, coloured crayons, pencils, felt tips.

polar bear

***Ursus maritimus***

The polar bear, *Ursus maritimus*, lives in the Arctic regions of the world and is a large predator. A solitary animal, it feeds off a wide variety of marine life, including seals and fish. The fur on its body is thought to be transparent, the hairs are hollow, letting in the heat of the sun and keeping the bear warm in the snow. The collective noun for a group of polar bears is an aurora.

1 animal solitary

tube-like hairs let sun's heat in and keep bear warm

aurora

it eats fish and seals

a very large predator in the Arctic region

# Bringing creativity into learning

By personalizing information, you take full ownership of a topic. For example, our solar system has nine planets: Mercury, Venus, Earth, Mars, Jupiter, Saturn, Uranus, Neptune and Pluto. Use any materials you have to hand – a wire coathanger, string, sticky tape, coloured card, pencils, crayons, felt tips – to make something that will help you remember the names of the planets.

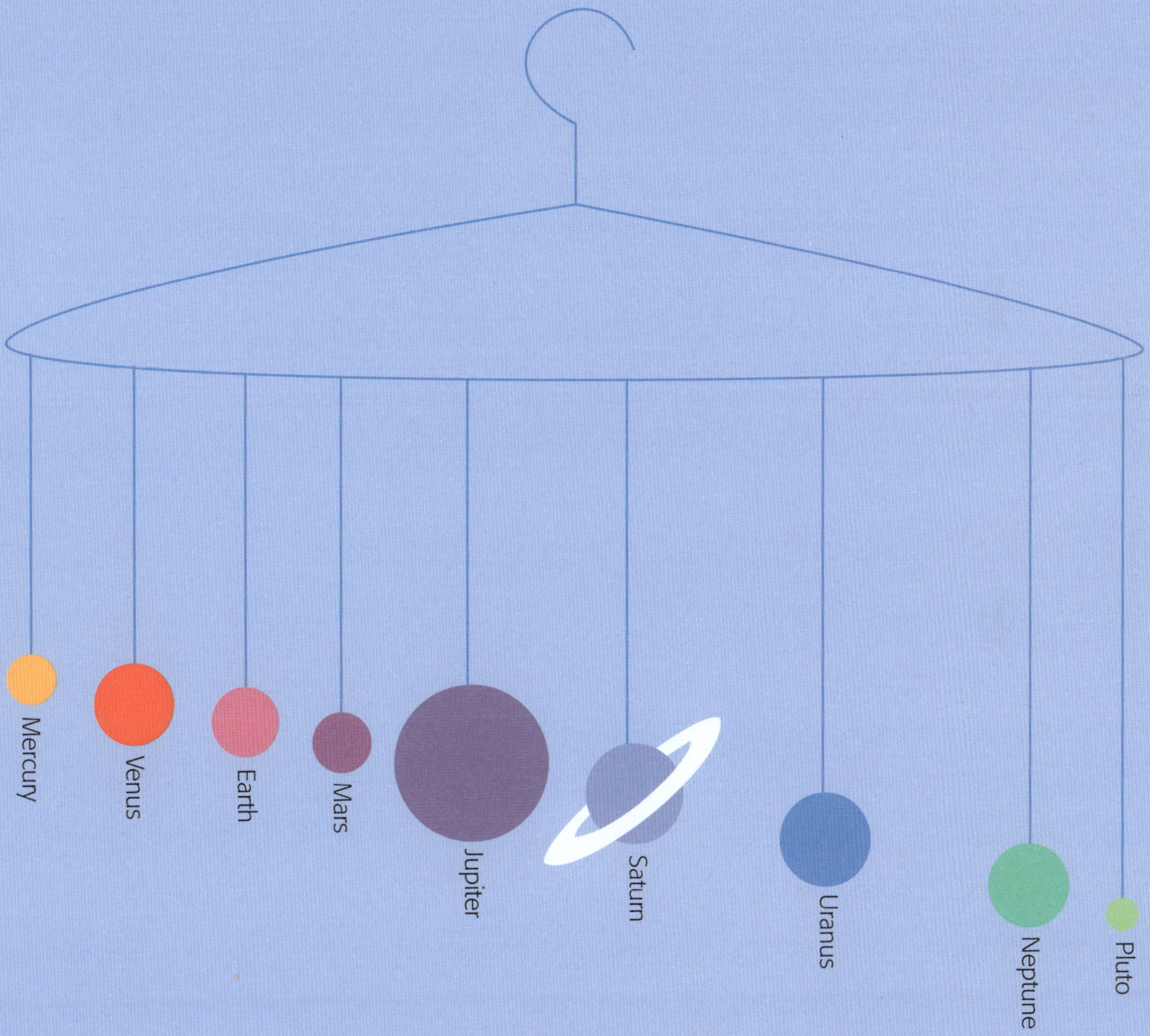


You could also make up your own mnemonic to remember the nine planets, like this:

**M**y **V**ery **E**nergetic **M**ind **J**ust **S**aved **U**ncle **N**athan's **P**rofits

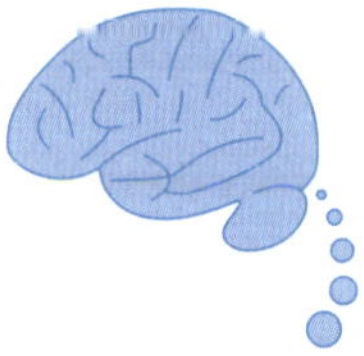

**Brilliant fact!**
Successful learning is all about seeing things in different ways and providing your child with the thinking tools to take any topic and work with it anywhere. People who have become brilliant in their fields have always known this. They have learnt to do things their own way and make knowledge their own.

never spring back to exactly what it thought or did before. New knowledge opens up new ways of thinking for the brain, taking it forwards. From now on, any time your child is presented with something to learn, their brain will automatically think, 'Hmm, I think I know a way I can learn this better and make this work more for me.' Progress!

## Maths through the looking glass

An example of someone doing things his own way is the brilliant mathematician John Nash, who won the Nobel Prize for his ground-breaking work. He found that he liked to work out his maths on windows using an easy wipe Chinagraph pencil. You can try it with your child (see 'Playing with numbers', opposite).

The beauty of working this way is that you can be right there in the middle of an equation and be looking for an answer; you may even have several ideas and write them all down. Try doing this on paper and you end up with lots of ugly scribbles that are rubbed out and distract you from keeping a clear line of thinking from where you started. But do it with a Chinagraph pencil and only the beauty of the maths remains because all you see when you have finished is the answers you got, minus any mess. Children are sensitive to making a mess in their exercise book, especially where they don't feel confident with a subject. So this is a great confidence booster.

## Riddles to re-juggle

Another technique that works well when children are trying to get a footing in a topic is to use riddles to re-juggle the information. Riddles help your child to:

- ★ Re-shape the information to make it more personal.
- ★ Find a different way of thinking about a new topic.
- ★ Develop problem-solving abilities.

All this combines to help children get into a topic better and at a deeper level, because they are not being passive but active thinkers. When children use riddles to learn something new, they are flexing their 'thinking muscles'.

Riddles have been around for centuries as a way to preserve information and pass down important knowledge. Practice makes

## Why work with a Chinagraph pencil on a mirror or window? checklist

✓ It takes away any fear of numbers.

✓ It allows a freedom that pen and paper can't do, because your child can experiment and not feel that the end result is just a mess.

✓ Numbers start to feel real and transparent, something to be played with and enjoyed.

✓ Novelty is something that helps the brain remember. When your child writes down a new formula in Chinagraph pencil on a bathroom mirror or window, the novelty of the experience makes it easier to remember.

# Playing with numbers

Stand at a window or mirror with your child armed with a Chinagraph pencil, which is water based and designed for people like restaurant owners to write their menus for the day on windows, then wipe off with a damp cloth. They are available at very little cost from all good office supply and stationery shops and come in all manner of colours, so you don't have to stick to white; you can use yellow, pink, blue and so on. Your child will also need a damp cloth.

**!! Health and safety come first.** As long as all windows and mirrors are strong and secure and your child understands that you don't have to press hard with a Chinagraph pencil – it glides on easily like paint – a great time can be had by all. Damaged windows or mirrors are not advised and always check that windows are double-glazed and secure and that only well fixed and secured wall mirrors are used. If in doubt, supervise your child at all times.

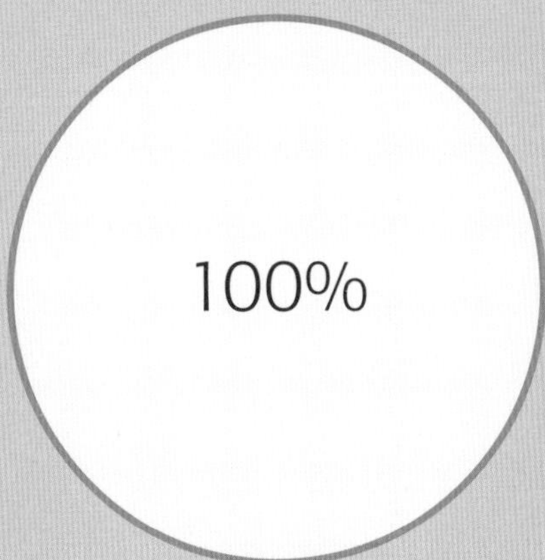


$\frac{1}{2} = 50\%$

What is $\frac{3}{4}$? ______________________

$\frac{1}{4} = 25\%$

**1** Look at the numbers above that relate to fractions and percentages. Then ask your child to make a list of any new maths rules or formulae that are being taught at school and need to be remembered.

**2** Ask your child to write the most important of these on the window or mirror. This then becomes a special place for your child to revisit and play with those particular numbers or formulae.

The mirror or window can be used for maths (or any other subject) homework where it would be useful to practise working out the answer before putting it neatly into a book for school. Enjoy!

# Developing thinking with riddles

Let your child read through this riddle and ask them to answer the questions underneath it. Remember from Chapter 1, that 'why?' questions are good for children's brain development and so, if after doing this activity, your child wants to find out more about the sun and the stars, then let that happen. That is brilliance at work!

**What's in a star?**
*Many of them come out at night,*
*But she does not,*
*High up in the heavens they live,*
*As does the glory of she,*
*Their beauty is mysterious,*
*All shiny white ablaze with silver sparkle*
*Theirs is the kingdom of night,*
*Hers the kingdom of day,*
*Her majesty more a brilliant gold*
*Her dazzle no less*
*Even though she is old*
*Surrounded by planets she holds court upon high,*
*See her as she smiles against the blue sky.*

**Who is she?**
**What is she?**
**And how is she different from the others?**

Once you have read through this together, pick another subject and make up a riddle. For example, it could be that you both choose to make a riddle about a rose, to help your child remember the different parts of a flower in biology. You can make a riddle from any subject as it trains your child's brain to think about topics in a different way.

you quicker at them – see 'Developing thinking with riddles', opposite, which is one that I made up to help a child learn that the sun is not a planet but a star in our solar system. Riddles are not only a brilliant learning tool, they are also a great way of developing a child's problem-solving abilities. So have a go!

## STEP 4

### Let children choose what works for them

Having a variety of strategies at their fingertips means that your child can bring any of them into play as required – your child is really starting to personalize their learning. When children do this, they are learning to use and choose what works for them. This places them in a very powerful position. When they do this, they are using skills that will not only help them across the school curricula but also throughout life.

## STEP 5

### Remind children that they are unique

The more children practise different techniques, the more they will begin to have the confidence not only to mix and match them but also to design and come up with a few of their own. Why not? Your child is unique and just as able as anyone to come up with great ideas that build upon the fact that they are now becoming an expert in how they think and learn. And when children begin to do this, it makes them very strong learners indeed.

## STEP 6

### Remain open to new ideas

Knowledge and research is forever moving on, and children can benefit from this as techniques and strategies can be influenced by new findings and discoveries. What we know about the brain and learning is an ongoing journey, not a static one, so keeping eyes and ears open to new ideas is important. However, now that you and your child are experts, you can afford to be more discerning than you might otherwise be when presented with new theories and so on. Remember that one size does not fit all when it comes to theories. Discussing new ideas with your child is a good thing. Encouraging children to take from new theories and ideas what they think is useful for them is even better. The most important thing is that children keep on doing what feels good and works for them.

## STEP 7

### Expert in personalized learning

Congratulations! You and your child are now experts. You know everything there is to know about personalized learning. Whenever you feel you need to revise things or remind your child how important it is to develop a good range of workable strategies, go through the exercises again in this chapter.

In the meantime, well done and make time for a pat on the back for both you and your child, you've done a great job.

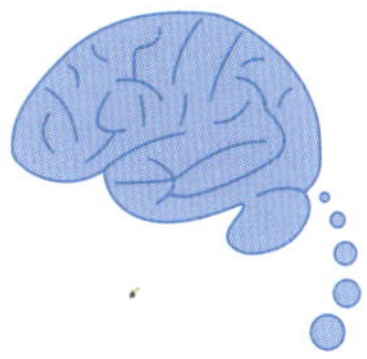

**Brilliant fact!**

The way children are taught to think and learn will change dramatically over the forthcoming decades. The main reason for this is that the knowledge from different fields is gradually converging within research centres around the world. This brings together findings about human development from areas such as neuroscience, computer modelling of networks to replicate the cognitive functions of the brain, education and the study of cultural approaches to learning derived from studies in anthropology. Last but not least, we can add to this list the impact that computers have had upon the way children learn.

My work is founded on findings in each of these fields and where they may lead learning in the future. All indications point to an era in which personalized learning will become the norm rather than the exception in the world's classrooms.

# The **route** to **success** 3

At the completion of Chapter 3 your child now has a major cornerstone in place for the foundations of success. It is extremely empowering for children to know how they learn best and being aware of the different techniques they can use to help them enjoy learning and make it fun. Your child now has begun to glimpse new possibilities and, with that, come windows of new opportunities for children to shine and show their abilities both inside and outside of school.

1 **Experiment with different ways of learning.** When finding out how your child learns best, don't start with the theories. Instead, start from the child and work from there. Children need to be in a position where they can become experts on how they learn best.

To reinforce the importance of exploring different ways of learning to find what suits your child, see 'When is an apple ever an apple?' on page 63 and 'Cultivating active learning' on page 70.

2 **Understand the current buzz words in learning.** Allowing children the opportunity to get inside learning theories and finding out what works for them is vital so they can take from these what works for them. When children have this knowledge they can begin to tailor-make a system of learning that really benefits them.

Visit today's hot buzz words in learning on pages 62–7. For a parents' evening, make a checklist of these to see what the school is using.

3 **Move beyond Mozart when it comes to 'brain music'.** Baroque music by composers such as Bach and Handel all work with the brain's own natural rhythms to help children focus and promote left-right brain connectivity.

Look at 'What's in a brain wave' on page 64 to see how the brain waves look when our brains are engaged in different kinds of activity.

4

**Understand the difference between acceleration and enrichment.** Acceleration is used when it may be appropriate for a child to skip a year's education; enrichment defines any activity inside or outside of school that deepens and broadens children's knowledge within any curricula area.

Approach acceleration from the informed viewpoint provided by the checklist on page 66.

5

**Let children get into the habit of rewarding and setting their own targets.** Target setting is used today in many schools. The trick is for children not to rely on others to set their targets. Once children are in the habit of doing this for themselves they are onto a winner.

Use the 'Target setting' checklist on page 67 to gently help your child master the art of target setting and achieving, and get them rewarding themselves with simple stickers to mark their success.

6

**Personalized learning is 21st-century learning.** Given that every child is as unique as their own thumbprint, it follows that if they can tailor-make a system of learning that works for them they stand a better chance of realizing their gifts.

Look at the 'Pyramid to tailor-made personal learning' on page 69. Follow each of the steps to enable your child to realize their gifts and abilities in full by knowing how they learn best.

7

**Encourage children to take ownership of their learning.** When children personalize their learning they begin to learn the importance of making knowledge their own. Whenever children encounter a new piece of information they need to know it is alright to rearrange it, play with it until they familiarize themselves with it.

'Playing with numbers' on page 73 and 'Developing thinking with riddles' on page 74 help children learn what generations of past brilliance already knew: great learning means making knowledge your own.

10 Your child is brilliant
Journey's end, journey's beginning

9 Living and learning
Making every day count!

8 Brilliant work space
Where brain training and focus meet

7 Goal setting and achieving
Teaching your child how to succeed

6 Working with schools
Cultivating the foundation for your child's future

5 Getting the best out of schools
What to look for beyond the 'tourist route'

# 4 Cutting tests down to size
## What every parent should know

3 How your child learns best
Different ways of learning

2 Discovering your child's gifts
Uncovering hidden treasures

1 Inside your child's brain
Understanding the technology

# 4

You don't need me to tell you that tests are an important part of all our children's lives at school. Over the past couple of decades, the testing industry has mushroomed and with it a lot of pressure on children. It is anticipated that despite moves by governments to the contrary, wherever children are in the world, they will continue to have a great deal of tests to sit through and succeed in.

We have already established from the previous chapter that when you are looking to discover your children's full range of gifts, there are limits to which abilities standard pen and paper tests can capture. However, it is important for parents to have a good understanding of how these national tests actually work, so that you can help your child get the best out of school. Forewarned is forearmed! By the end of this chapter you will have a good grasp of each of the following:

★ How to find out what tests your child has done and why.

★ What kinds of ability tests exist and what they are designed to test.

★ How to break down test scores and understand them.

★ How to get the most out of test scores to inform future learning.

★ Why tests are not foolproof.

★ How to help your child prepare effectively for tests.

# Which **tests** has your **child** done and **why?**

Schools today rely heavily on tests to categorize and streamline students from an early age so that they can spot strengths and weaknesses in children, who can then get the support they need. This aspect of testing is great in theory. The trouble is that whichever way you test for ability early on, there is a risk attached to it due to the practical matter of human development. Not every child blooms at the same stages. In fact, all indications are that children and people bloom at different ages and stages. When and how children are tested, therefore, can affect their chances in different ways. For example, if when children are tested they aren't at their best, for a whole host of reasons, the test scores that stay on their files don't really reflect the true nature of their abilities. Just a few months later and they may achieve a very different score. You see the problem.

Many schools work hard to counterbalance this by making sure that teacher assessments and observations are taken into account when judgements are made about a child's ability. But the fact remains that tests, love them or hate them, occupy a centre stage in every child's school career. So it is practical for everyone's purposes that you know precisely which tests your child has done, when and why.

This is not being a pushy parent; it is just accepting the important fact that the system is driven by tests. It therefore stands to reason that to get the best out of any system, you are better placed to do so if you understand it.

The easiest way to begin to do this is to jot down the fact-finding checklist, opposite, for your next parents' evening and ask your child's teacher. Alternatively, if you find that your child's teachers are particularly strapped for time, it is advisable to acknowledge this and try to set aside an appointment with them. It is not a new observation that many teachers and parents around the world are of the joint view that there are too many tests right now. So don't be surprised if what you thought was going to be a short conversation with your child's teacher, turns out to be a very long and rewarding one. There is going to be lots to talk about and a lot to find out.

## SUBJECT TESTS

In class, teachers regularly set tests for individual subjects across the curriculum that your child is studying. These are pretty straightforward to understand because they focus upon a term's or year's work in a given topic area, for example, science, maths or history. Feedback from these kinds of tests is usually very thorough from schools because you get two sets of complementary information, one is quantitative and the other qualitative:

* Subject test score (quantitative).
* The teacher's observations (qualitative).

This allows both you and your child to have a more rounded view of where strengths lie and which areas need more focus and attention.

## ABILITY TESTS

Worldwide, these kinds of tests are sometimes used in schools. They don't test subject areas specifically, but if your child's school has used them, you will find your child will have been given an average score made up usually of the following three areas that they were tested upon.

* Non-verbal
* Verbal
* Quantitative.

**Non-verbal questions** typically comprise abstract sets of geometric and numerical symbols. These types of questions involve children using logic and reason to figure out relationships and patterns within and between things. For an example of this type of question, see page 82.

**Verbal questions** focus on testing children's ability in comprehension and language. For example, they may get questions such as:

*If rabbit is to carrot, then monkey is to: potato, burger, banana, cake*

The child is then asked to circle the correct answer, in this case, of course, banana. The principle underpinning this sort of question lies in detecting the relationship at any given time between the first and second object. This becomes progressively harder as the relationship between the first object and the second becomes more difficult to detect. How well children do will be dependent upon how well read they are and how much vocabulary they have amassed. For example:

*Herd is to cows as muster is to: ravens, sheep, peacocks, tigers*

The relationship here is between collective nouns and what they describe; hence the answer is peacocks because muster is the collective noun for peacocks, just as a herd is the collective noun for cows.

**Quantitative questions** focus upon numerical ability and normally relate to the maths curriculum the children would be expected to be following at that time. Here is an example of a quantitative question:

If Leila had five oranges and she gave two to Bethan, one to Robin and bought two more oranges at the grocery store, how many oranges would Leila have?

## **Parent fact-finding** checklist 1

✓ How many tests has my child taken so far?

✓ When did these take place?

✓ Are all these tests subject based?

✓ If so, which subjects has my child been tested in to date?

✓ If not, what other kinds of tests have been administered?

✓ How many of these other tests have been administered?

✓ What was the purpose of each?

✓ Which areas did they cover?

# Examples of non-verbal questions on tests

1. What comes next?

**a**

**b**

**c**

2. What comes next?

**a**

**b**

**c**

**For the answers, see page 160**

The answer is, of course, four oranges. The purpose of the question is to test the child's thinking when it comes to keeping a track of what sum has been taken away and added to the original number of oranges that Leila had. Questions get more complicated than this, and involve other areas of mathematics usually reflecting the age of the child and the curriculum they will have been expected to cover at that age. Practice on these types of questions, as with the other sections in these kinds of tests, does help. But knowing what the section entails is the first step to being able to tackle them.

### How ability test scores work

The good thing about tests used universally is that they do consider a range of abilities. The bad thing is that usually the scores are reported as one whole score. Test scores naturally appear authoritative and impressive, but the truth is that whole scores generated from such tests can unintentionally be a little misleading if you don't know how that figure was arrived at. For example, a child may have done exceptionally well in one area of the test, such as the non-verbal section, but on all other areas, has not done very well. Most children's scores tend to have sections where they have done better in one area than in others. In other words, if you are given an overall score, that figure just represents an average across all the tests. It doesn't indicate to you precisely where your child's strengths and abilities actually lie, or where there may be particular areas that need addressing.

So, if you have a parents' evening coming up, this may be a good time to add to the checklist provided in the previous section before you go (see right).

Most schools will already have on record somewhere a full breakdown of each section score for your child. In practical terms, on a busy parents' evening it may not be entirely productive or convenient for a teacher to dive off and locate your child's file in the locked cabinet of the head teacher's office. You may have to wait a little. But it will be worth the wait, because inside that breakdown of scores is a treasure trove of knowledge that will enable you to find out what your child's strengths are, and which areas need to be worked on and practised so your child can succeed fully in any future similar tests. In addition, knowing when those tests are going to take place and what kinds of sections are going to be on them is key to finding practice questions that will help your child succeed.

## **Parent fact-finding** checklist 2

✓ On any of the tests that my child has done, are there different sections?

✓ Which kinds of sections are they?

✓ What did they test?

✓ Do you have any examples?

✓ What was the actual breakdown of scores?

✓ What did my child get in each section?

✓ What do you think that tells you?

✓ Which areas then would you say are my child's strongest?

✓ Are there any areas that you think we need to look at?

✓ When will my child be doing more tests?

✓ What are these tests?

✓ Can I get any practice books?

✓ Where can I get them?

# Universal tricks for universal tests

Throughout the world, various kinds of ability tests are used. However, education systems are converging globally and so there is also a convergence of the different types of questions that appear on a variety of ability tests for children. Many of the questions used test children's abilities to think in different ways. And there are some general 'tricks of the trade' that once children are aware of can help them prepare and succeed on such tests.

Practice in thinking in different ways like this is brain training in action: it is teaching your child how to crack different kinds of mental challenges. To help your child do this, I have provided some common types of the different questions that are used.

## Challenge type 1: random number values for letters

In this form of code breaking, letters are given random values rather than following the alphabet rule: 'A' cannot be assumed to be '1', just as 'Z' can't be assumed to be '26'. So in this type of question, there is usually a crib for the children to give them some indication of what they need to be thinking about to crack the problem.

In each case, a crib is given in the first line up of letters and numbers. A key trick to learn here is that no two cribs are the same.

Complete the missing word in each case:

**BEANBAG KITE**
4235438 7692 4 6 8
— — —

**RABBIT RUN HARRY**
726604 798 52773 6 9 8
— — —

**BLUE ROSE RED**
1702 6392 625 5 2 2 6
— — — —

Now try making up some of your own!

**For the answers, see page 160**

## Challenge type 2: alphabet number switches

The most straightforward way to break codes is to use a staple trick: apportion numbers to alphabet letters. This method operates on the fact that if you set out the numbers of the alphabet, they each have a numerical value, as shown here.

Give a number to each letter of the alphabet, e.g.:

| A | B | C | D | E | F | G | H | I | J | K | L | M | N | O | P | Q | R |
|---|---|---|---|---|---|---|---|---|---|---|---|---|---|---|---|---|---|
| 1 | 2 | 3 | 4 | 5 | 6 | 7 | 8 | 9 | 10 | 11 | 12 | 13 | 14 | 15 | 16 | 17 | 18 |

| S | T | U | V | W | X | Y | Z |
|---|---|---|---|---|---|---|---|
| 19 | 20 | 21 | 22 | 23 | 24 | 25 | 26 |

Once this 'rule' is understood, it is possible to break the codes to solve the problems in the activity, e.g.:

**Y + Z = 51**　　**K + T = 31**　　**Q + R = 35**

Using this principle, what is the message hidden in the following code?

**9　1 13　22 5 18 25　19 13 1 18 20!**

_　_ _　_ _ _ _　_ _ _ _ _

What do these numbers spell?

**23 9 14 14 5 18**

_ _ _ _ _ _

**2 18 9 12 12 9 1 14 20**

_ _ _ _ _ _ _ _ _

Now make some up of your own!

**For the answers, see page 160**

# Challenge type 3: pattern detection

This type of question is very popular on universal tests for ability. It is all about relationships between things. It challenges children to detect any patterns in the questions. The range and type of pattern detection-type questions can take in a mixture of abstract objects and number sequences. Look at these activities and see what you can find out.

1. What comes next?

**a** 40 **b** 29 **c** 80 **d** 47

2. Which is the odd one out?

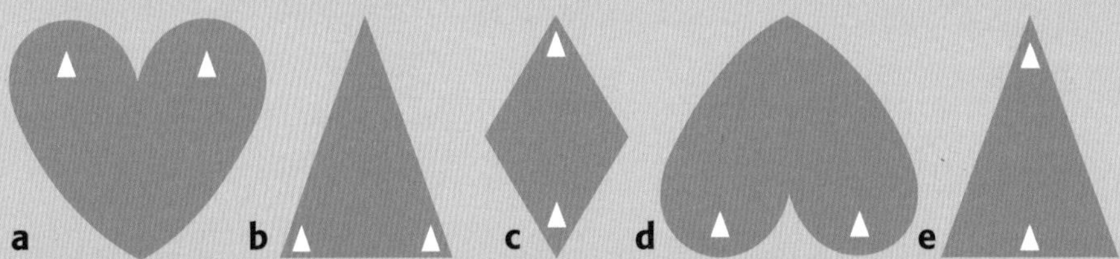

**a** **b** **c** **d** **e**

3. What comes next?

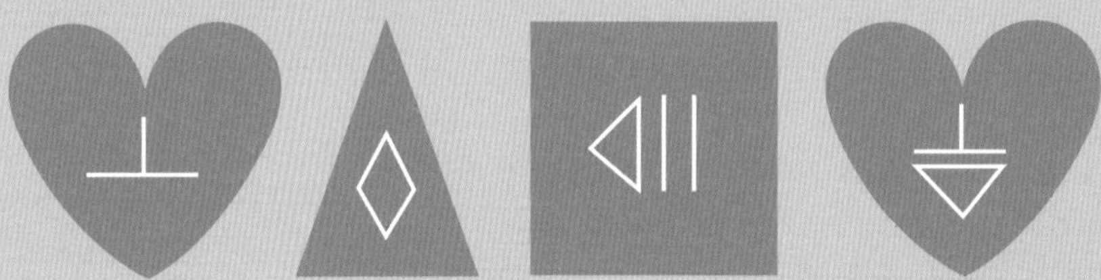

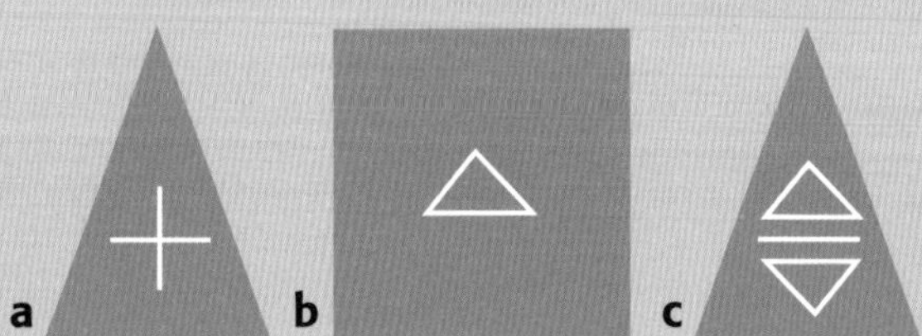

**a** **b** **c**

4. What comes next?

| 4 | 13 | 40 | 121 | ? |
|---|---|---|---|---|

**a** 364 **b** 170 **c** 129 **d** 133

5. Which is the odd one out?

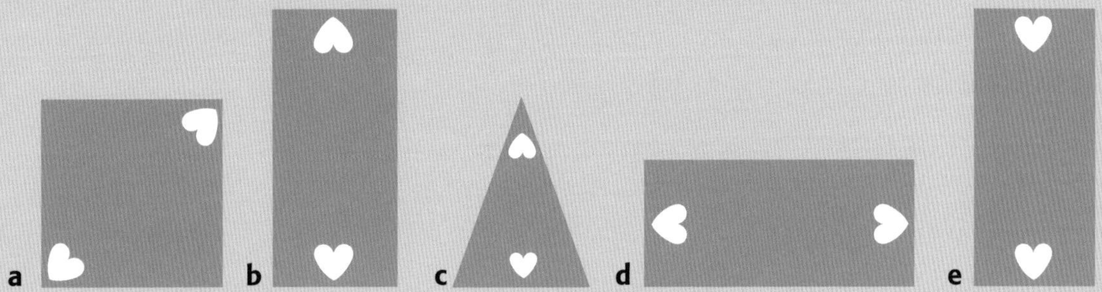


6. Which comes next?

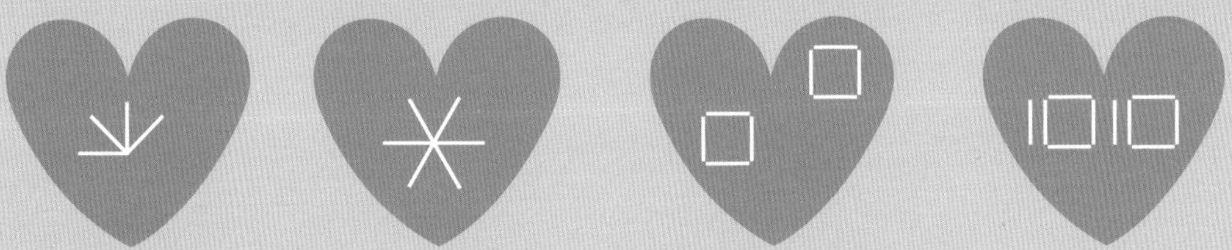

**For the answers, see page 160**

# Why **tests** are **not foolproof**

In my work with children, I use a wide range of challenges, including the concepts and ideas covered in this book. I use as diverse a range of challenges as possible simply because tests are not foolproof in detecting a child's individual abilities. To illustrate just how important it is not to rely too heavily on one kind of test in looking at your own child, let me share with you the story of Josh.

> *Josh was in junior school and had just gone through a battery of national tests and unfortunately flunked the whole lot. Thankfully, his teachers were very much on the ball. They had noted that he had a very low boredom threshold, was highly creative and imaginative when it came to class projects and responded positively to learning new things. When they put all this together from their observations, not withstanding that he had flunked his tests, they were clear about one thing: Josh must be a very bright little boy and needed to be on the school's gifted and talented list. And when I met Josh I was convinced they were absolutely right, Josh had masses of creative energy.*

## THE IMPORTANCE OF CREATIVITY

There is no definitive test for creativity and yet it is this human mental energy that drives us forward in every known field. It is for this reason that in challenges with children I include lots of opportunity for them to show off their creativity. The only known measure in psychology for creativity is not very imaginative – it is the 'How many things can you do with a brick?' test! I tend to think that children are attracted to things a little more exciting than a brick, so in the series I challenge them to think of different ways to put a cuddly toy or some such other novel item to use. They love it and you and your child can try this at home – see 'Practising creative thinking', opposite.

National tests taken in school are there not just to test children's abilities, but also to provide a form of measurement for government targets. Such measurements depend upon using statistics for quality control, which by their very nature require tangible figures. Imagination and creativity are not easily reduced to numbers and so cannot be given a precise number value. As a result, they have been squeezed out of the school testing system.

**Brilliant fact!**

The reason why so many tests are not foolproof is that research has found that where really bright children are faced with the kinds of questions that appear on standard tests, they actually find them too easy and so over-complicate the question – leading, ironically, to a fail when really this is a potentially strong indication that they are actually very bright.

# Practising creative thinking

Choose a favourite cuddly toy or any household item and let your child see how many ideas they come up with about what they could do with the object. The aim is to let their imagination run riot. It is great fun, costs nothing and develops creative thinking.

**How many things can you think of that you could do with this cuddly dragon?**

Here are some ideas to get you started. You could use him...

★ as a doorstop
★ as a pillow or
★ as a stool to sit on.

# Helping your child succeed in tests

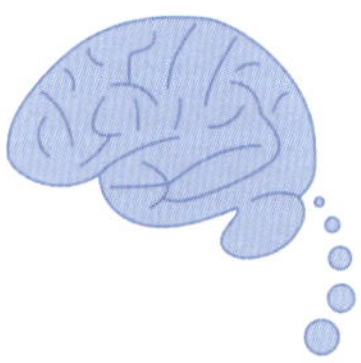

**Brilliant fact!**

Armed with the three checklists on page 91, children can benefit from really knowing about tests. This helps take the fear out of tests and gives them ownership. When it comes to revision, children will also know how to attack a test and succeed.

I recently did some research on the statistical measures that have been used to assess quality control in education, and found that they are not dissimilar to those used in bottling factories. While there is, of course, a very important need for checks to be kept on quality standards, the problem with using statistics like this is that whichever way you look at them, they do tend to treat children as though they are static and passive numbers in a statistical equation. Whereas, as we all know, children's brain development and abilities are not static as a bottle might be as it moves through a bottling plant.

Children are exciting, active, diverse, multi-talented and, above all, highly creative and imaginative individuals. Part of the challenge of school for children today is to learn how to cope effectively with the testing culture. So here are some techniques to help your child succeed in tests.

## TECHNIQUE 1

**Overcoming a fear of the unknown**

The first barrier to children's success in tests is fear of the unknown. Tests can feel elusive and far removed, so ensure your child understands how to become a sleuth about forthcoming tests. Children need to be bold and not afraid to ask their teacher to find out as much as they can about what lies ahead. Share the 'Overcoming fear' checklist, opposite, and you will both learn a lot more about what a test actually is.

## TECHNIQUE 2

**Understanding the marking system**

Another barrier to children's success is that they often don't understand how a given test actually works in terms of balance for marks and percentages. Strategy is everything when it comes to exams. You can have all the knowledge and worked really hard, but if you don't know how to net the biggest marks, and which parts of the test carry those large percentages, then you can miss out. So ask your child to find out: what matters most on this test?

The secret for passing exams is often 90 per cent strategy, 10 per cent knowledge. Some children work really hard and others have only a bit of knowledge and come out with exactly the same mark. The only reason this should happen is the extent to which a child understands how the marking system is actually weighted in the different sections of a test.

## TECHNIQUE 3

**Taking ownership**

By helping your child to become a super sleuth in tests, you are also helping your child to take responsibility for them. Here it is important to remember what you learned about the importance of ownership in children's learning on pages 68–9. Give children ownership in something and they are more likely to be self-motivated to work at it. The 'Taking ownership' checklist, opposite, helps children take charge of tests, which further helps them to be more confident by understanding the test.

I cannot emphasize enough the importance of children checking if there are any sections in a test that particularly need to be focused on, either because they need practice in that particular area, or because a particular section may carry extra marks. This is the information that children usually find out about after the test, but to do well they need to find out about this BEFORE the test. To ensure this ground is covered, sit down together and find out as much as you can about the particular test you are focusing on. If you are lucky, there may be no areas to think about in particular, but more often than not, there will be one area that does need some extra work. So find out what it is and get cracking on that now.

### TECHNIQUE 4

**Revising successfully**

Everyone revises differently and from what you have already learned in this book, your child will now have a range of successful strategies for personalized learning, covered on pages 68–75. Nevertheless, there are some basic rules (see 'Revision strategy must-haves', right) that are the foundation of every successful exam story.

Children who are aware of the information in this chapter, have a much better chance of passing tests or exams. They can also begin to see tests as something to do battle with and win and, in many cases, children only need one win to let them see tests as something they can actually enjoy. Depending on the success your child has had with tests to date, this may seem a near or far distant outcome. But have faith and trust in the fact that I have seen many a transformation in test results using the simple but effective strategies described in this chapter. Good luck!

## Checklists
## Overcoming fear

✓ When are we due to have the test?

✓ How long is the test?

✓ Is it a school test, have you set it?

✓ Is it a national test, what is it called?

✓ What kinds of things will it be testing us on?

## Taking ownership

✓ How many sections are on the test?

✓ Which things do I especially need to revise or think about?

✓ How are the different sections weighted?

✓ Do some sections get more marks than others?

✓ If so, which ones?

✓ How is the final score made up?

✓ Do you think there are any sections that I particularly need to focus on?

## Revision strategy must-haves

✓ Always do the worst first. If there is a topic that you find tricky – then that is the one to start with.

✓ Know how long you have to revise.

✓ Draw up a realistic plan of working that includes breaks. The maximum number of minutes people can usually focus hard is 45 minutes. So build in breaks at regular 45-minute intervals at least.

✓ During breaks, get some fresh air, try to eat healthily and drink plenty of water. Don't slump in front of the TV; if you do that, you can easily lose hours!

✓ Reward yourself so that you set up in your brain a positive cycle that links working hard with good results.

# The **route** to **success** 4

When your child knows how tests work and how to prepare for them, you are on to an instant winner all the way. Dependent upon your past experience of tests, you may or may not believe it when I say that many a test can actually be fun when your child understands the rules to win. It's just like everything else: easy when you know how.

1 **Learn about the different types of tests for ability.** Ability tests are a common feature of many education systems globally so it is a good idea to understand how they work and what kinds of things they are actually testing.

Using the 'Parent fact-finding checklist 1' on page 81 enables you to find out which, if any, tests your child has done at school.

2 **Break down average scores on tests to find out what they actually reveal.** Always understand how the final mark was arrived at for any test your child has done. Average scores are less useful than having scores broken down so that you can see which areas your child did well in and which ones, if any, require attention.

Use the 'Parent fact-finding checklist 2' on page 83 to get inside any test your child may have done and find out exactly how it works and what it can tell you.

3

**Practise the tricks used in ability tests.** Universally, ability tests used in education systems share some basic features: such as non-verbal, verbal and quantitative type questions. There are key ways of thinking that regularly come up on these kinds of tests and once children learn some of the tricks, they can begin to think in a way that helps them succeed.

With your child, work through the challenges on pages 82 and 84–7. Each of these teaches you a different trick that once children know, they will never forget and can use again.

4

**Success in any test or exam is as much about strategy as it is about knowledge.** A child can work very hard but not do as well as they justly deserve simply because they don't understand about exam strategy. Children need to know how a test works and how it will be marked, so that once they are in that exam hall they have a sure fire plan for success.

Share with your child the checklists 'Overcoming fear', 'Taking ownership' and 'Revision strategy must-haves' on page 91 to help your child master exams.

5

**Remind your child that their creativity and imagination are important, but that these things cannot be captured in full on any test.** Creative thinking and imagination remain difficult to test and yet highly important in any field of human endeavour, particularly in the global knowledge economy where innovation and ideas of young people generate wealth and jobs.

'Practising creative thinking' on page 89 is a great way for children to develop this area, gain confidence in sharing ideas and is fun to do.

# 5 Getting the best out of schools

## What to look for beyond the 'tourist route'

# 5

The word 'school' conjures up many an image in the mind's eye. For most people it means thinking back to their own school days, times when they laughed and times when they cried. Buddies you had such great times with, but you can't quite remember their names now. Your first sweetheart, teachers who made you laugh, and that uniform you never did quite like or maybe you secretly were proud to wear. And last, but not least, getting dressed up in your finest, all set to paint the town red with your friends the day you left.

However you remember time at school, it will quite likely have changed a lot since you were running in and out of those big gates. Education worldwide is an area that has recently undergone unprecedented and rapid change. This change has occurred due to three key events that are shaping the future of education and schools: the impact of the global knowledge economy; research from neuroscience, and the information technology boom.

Things are not what they used to be, are they? And neither are schools. The way in which education is funded by governments around the world is also becoming an issue on many politicians' agendas. The manner in which schools were originally set up did not take into account, for example, the impact that laptops, white boards and online learning have had on children. These present exciting opportunities for learning, but they all come at a cost: massive investment. But whichever way this investment is to be made, there is no doubt about one thing: the role of education in the global knowledge economy is paramount to the future success of children.

In my work with schools and education ministries from Beijing to London, the emphasis is on developing new ways of thinking about education for children by investing in new technology and new research about the brain.

White boards have replaced blackboards, giving rise to great possibilities in the classroom for teachers to develop interactive lessons. Chinese is on the agenda in primary schools to welcome in the new era of exciting possibilities for the world economy as the Far East comes into its own.

Innovation and creativity are the words on everyone's lips from the newly emerging economies of central Europe and Asia. The reason is simple: in the global knowledge economy, ideas count. Ideas generate jobs and create wealth for future generations. Hence young people who are well educated and know how to harness their brain's creative energy are best placed to make the most of the global knowledge economy.

More than this, children today are more likely to take advantage of online learning, with the internet making resources accessible to them from around the world.

All of these facts, plus the impact of neuroscience discussed throughout this book, means that education ministries are beginning to think about schools in a whole new light. The world is going through a renaissance of thinking about learning, and do you know what? From my experience of working with schools, this is all great news for our children. These are exciting times for your child to be going to school.

All that remains to do now, of course, is to help you and your child get the best out of those school years, and a big part of that is to know what to look for when considering different schools.

## CONSIDERING SCHOOLS

When it comes to looking at schools, if there is one thing that can hamper parents in making an informed decision, it is a lack of knowledge about how schools actually operate. More often than not, as with any field, unless we are in it, we tend to work from assumptions and ideas, limited experience and bits of things we might hear from relatives or news items. This leaves us with an incomplete jigsaw of knowledge. And there never seems to be anyone around who can bring all this information together for you when you need it most.

This chapter is designed to remedy that, and in the process remove some of the mystery and fears, so that together you and your child can make the best possible choices for the future.

## TACKLING THE 'UNKNOWNS'

Starting a school can be a nail-biting experience for children and parents alike. This is not only because it is a big step, akin to buying a house or getting married, but because worry can arise due to the range of the 'unknowns' that parents can often face:

★ Will my child fit in at this school?

★ Are the staff going to be nice?

★ Can I expect my child to do well at this particular school?

★ Do I need to think about getting out my chequebook and paying?

★ Or am I better off at this local state-funded school?

Knowing how to tackle these unknowns and replacing them with some facts is the first step in being able to find out which school will suit your child best. As you read the rest of this chapter, you will learn how to sift the facts from the fiction in all that you are told about schools and education, making any decision about your child's school that much easier. To start our journey, I am going to grasp that mother of all nettles in the 'great education debate' the world over: is fee-paying education better than state-funded education?

## TO PAY OR NOT TO PAY?

I have started with this issue because this is the question that is always asked of me whenever I am a 'captive expert', namely 35,000 feet up, boxed into a window seat on a plane for a 13-hour flight or strapped into my dentist's chair with a mouthful of cotton wool. So here goes. If you really want the truth about which is best, then you need to wipe all assumptions out of your mind and focus on this one reality: forget the labels. Labels are pretentious and gloss over a multitude of things when it comes to assessing what might be a 'good school' for your child.

When looking to assess schools, make it your mantra that you will always look at the individual school. I have witnessed some great fee-paying schools and some not so great fee-paying schools. Similarly, I have witnessed some great state-funded and some not so great state-funded schools. So, start with the actual school and work from there.

> *Pockets of excellence in schools come in many different shapes and forms and appearances can be deceptive. One of the best schools I ever encountered was a refugee school set up in a disused army barracks in the middle of a desert. What made it so special? The answer is simple: the commitment and expertise of the staff and management – they wanted to do a great job and they did. Moral of the story: appearances can be deceptive.*

## Reading statistics

But what about statistics meted out about exam results every year? Don't statistics appear to indicate that fee-paying schools have the lead over state-funded schools in exam performance? Broadly speaking, of course, the answer is yes. But 'appear' is the operative word. School exam results form an impressive bunch of numbers based on taking an average of every child's performance. But such statistical averages don't tell you how each child actually arrived at their own final result.

A child's individual result, regardless of whether they attended a fee-paying or state-funded school, can arise from many different factors that operate outside a school's remit. For example, it is not a new observation that many children at key exam stages, either within fee-paying or state-funded schools, may take on an evening tutor to bolster their marks in a given subject area. However, such data is not worked into the national statistics, but it is easy to see how 'invisible data' like this, if worked into such statistics, might prove interesting. For this reason, averages of school exam results are less informative for parents than actually looking at each school itself and ascertaining just how that school might best serve their individual child's needs.

## What are you looking for?

The question you and your child need to ask yourselves is: 'What exactly is it that we want out of a school?' This may seem an obvious question, but when people ask themselves this, not everyone, in fact, wants exactly the same things. Before you set off to find out about your 'ideal school' it is good to know what it is that you and your child are really looking for in a school. When children are only toddlers, the bulk of that decision will rest on you. But as they get older, they have a mind of their own and have their own views. So, when you are deciding what you are looking for, make it a joint decision.

If you don't decide what exactly it is that you want out of a school before you go off looking, you can end up making the wrong choices for all of the right reasons. It's a bit like when you go out shopping. Ever gone out vaguely to buy a pair of shoes and ended up coming back with a washing machine instead? Education today, despite all the controversy that surrounds it, does offer a broad range of options in that no two schools are ever exactly the same. Knowing what to ask and not being vague about this when you are visiting the school is the key to putting your and your child's mind at peace and this is what the next section in this chapter is concerned with.

# Taking the **'how can this work for us?'** route

So, you have arrived at the school open day. The principal is charming. The school is shining with wall displays and polished floors. You have heard great things about this school. But the question remains, what's it like?

Depending upon how confident schools are, they will or will not be happy for you to wander off the tourist route. The 'tourist route' is what inspectors, visitors and parents are typically presented with whenever a school is putting itself out on display to the public. This is fine, as long as you remember that playing the tourist is not the same as being a full-time client of this school, which is what the visit is actually all about for you and your child. If you find yourself slipping into polite tourist mode, snap out of it.

This visit is the one time you are ever likely to be able to ask a number of questions that hold the keys to your child's future. So, as you step through the front doors, remember what you came to find out. Not everything will be on the set tourist route, and at times you will have to move tactfully away from it to find out what you want.

Using the checklist 'How to find out everything you need to know on school open days', opposite, should help you stay on track and also find out all that you need to know to help you make your decision before it is time to leave.

Starting a new school can be a nerve-racking time for both parents and children, but much of the tension can be diffused when many of the 'unknowns' are exchanged for facts. In an ideal world, education would not be as filled with the complications that it now seems to involve. However, as it stands, our choices will always be affected by personal circumstance and whatever set of rules governments have operating at any given time. But, like any new venture, setting out at least with a full understanding of the terrain we are operating in is the first important step in knowing how to get the best out of it.

I have seen children succeed and achieve their dreams from all kinds of different schools, backgrounds, circumstances, cultural heritage and creed. The key factor behind that success is that children and parents understand how to get the best out of the system they are operating in at any given time.

This chapter has given you the foundation and tools to help you do that too. Here is wishing you and your child the best of success every step of the way.

**Brilliant fact!**

Even if your choice of school is limited, by finding out as much as you can about the school your child is attending or likely to attend, you then stand a better chance of understanding how to work with the school to get the best out of it in the future.

# How to find out everything you need to know on school open days

## TIP 1

**Departments are just as important as whole schools**

All schools have particular departments that shine out. This is down to the fact that schools are made up of staff and, as with any area where people come together, some teams, regardless of resource or other factors, are just great, others are just average. Whichever department shines out in the school you are looking at is likely to reflect an area that your child will benefit from very much. Find out which departments seem to have key personnel that are making things happen in their school and get chatting to them. Visit their classrooms. Ask all staff you meet, regardless of what they teach:

★ What future projects are they planning for their students?

★ How long have they been at the school?

★ Do they like what they do?

As they respond, ask yourself do they look excited and interested in what they do?

## TIP 2

**Find out whether the turnover of staff in the school is high or low**

How the staff feel affects how your child will feel. Where the staff turnover is low it is a strong indication that staff and management are working well together. And when that happens there is a greater likelihood that staff will be happier; and when they are happy, then children are more likely to feel happier in their learning too. A low staff turnover also indicates that there is likely to be more continuity in work year on year. You may find out that there are higher staff turnover areas in some departments than others. If so, find out why. As you do this, you will begin to build up a sense of how the school operates in general.

## TIP 3

**Check out the exam results, which are available in printed and online format in many schools – but also look for the 'value added'**

'Value added' are those things, such as after-school clubs, that cannot easily be measured, but which can make a very big difference to your child's happiness and success at school. Also find out how the school deals with bullying. Particularly when children are just starting the school, find out if the school cultivates an inclusive, warm message so that all children feel valued. What does it do to put this into action? Ask for some practical examples. In other words, make sure that mission statements are not just good intentioned waffle, but that they are made a reality for the children in the school.

## TIP 4

**Look at the wall displays – are they new? Is this business as usual or unusual?**

On open days, often schools will use students to escort parents along the 'tourist route' and manage display areas along the way. Displays can look really fantastic and colourful, adding interest to every classroom or corridor wall they adorn. Good, well-kept displays with lots of student work on show are a key indication that teaching is vibrant and alive in a school – they can mean: 'Hey, look! We are really proud and excited by learning and what we do in this school.' If they look brand new on an open day, they can also mean: 'Hey, look! This is what some poor soul had to knock together at Olympic scrambling speed late last night to make this corner look good for you!' Is this business as usual or just for show?

The best people to ask are the students – after all, they are in there every day. Also look at the displays. Is there a fair mixture of brand new ones and some with their corners slightly dog-eared? A mixture is healthy; all new smacks of an overheated staple gun the night before.

## TIP 5

**Chat to other visiting parents**

Chat is good as it lets you find out about the other parents and also lets you have an opportunity to share and find out more information. So use any opportunity to do this. It need not be heavy chat, just gentle banter to break the ice and get to know other parents better.

## TIP 6

**Let your child chat to other prospective children, and also the children who are already at the school**

This will help give your child a sense of what it is like to attend the school on a social basis, as well as glean any other bits of useful information that may come out of talking to the other children.

## TIP 7

**Talk to the principal, asking 'What are the main strengths of the school?'**

Look for incisive responses with a clear indication that they know what they want and where they are going with the school. Also look how they respond to your questions. Are they enthusiastic and approachable? This will give you an indication of how to approach the principal in the future, when or if needs be.

## TIP 8

**Establish what the extra-curricular activity is like in the school**

It is important to provide children with additional enrichment in a variety of areas that they might like to take part in. Check if there is a wide range of subject areas or interests available, from sport to chess, science and drama. If you are looking at a state-funded school, this may occasionally come at a small extra charge but, in most cases, there is little or no charge. However, if you are looking at a fee-paying school, this is a good point to get down to finances. There is the main set menu in such schools that covers the primary subject and curriculum areas, and then there is the á la carte menu. Don't underestimate the cost of the latter. This will include things like extra music lessons, ballet, photography, for example. Making use of these extras may be important for your child's social as well as academic success in the school. So you need to know about any additional costs expected to inform your budget and decision.

### TIP 9

**Find out how your child as a new arrival to the school will be supported**

Most schools will have a very strong pastoral support structure for new arrivals. To get the best out of this you need to know who are the key members of staff. Once you have located them, open days are a great way to introduce yourself and your child and get to know the staff. Make a note of their names and contact numbers.

### TIP 10

**Step up**

If you still have any nagging questions, then ask them. If you find that a certain teacher you were interested in speaking to isn't available or you run out of time on the open day, make a note of his or her name and see if you can arrange a follow-up appointment.

## **Looking at schools** checklist

✓ When you attend open days, remember not to fall into 'tourist' mode, you are there to find out as much as you can.

✓ Think about schools as being like organizations with different departments and different strengths.

✓ No matter what your preconceptions are about different types of school, remember that you and your child's needs are best served by looking at the individual strengths of any given school.

✓ Find out which departments stand out and why.

✓ Talk to staff and ask questions.

✓ Use the opportunity to meet the principal and ask more questions.

# The **route** to **success** 5

In today's global economy, the power of knowledge has never been more important. Wherever you are in the world and no matter how wide or narrow your school choice, by reading this chapter you are better equipped to make an informed decision. And this can only help your child get the best out of school.

1 **Look at the school itself and forget labels.** There are pockets of excellence in different kinds of schools everywhere. All schools, regardless of the sector they serve, aim to operate much as you might expect a successful corporation to.

Take the mystery out of any school you are looking at by 'Tackling the "unknowns"' and working through the bullets on page 96.

2 **Look beyond statistical data when considering school performance.** Statistics are only numerical calculations. What is and is not included in the data largely determines their outcome. And not everything a school achieves or excels in can be measured by statistics. Look at examination performance but also consider the factors that may have resulted in that outcome.

Check 'Reading statistics' page 97 to help you move beyond only thinking about performance data. Consider also the impact of different factors that can affect individual student performance.

3 **Bear in mind the all-important question: what are you looking for?** This may seem an obvious question to ask yourself and your child when looking at schools, but it is a good one to ask, particularly when surrounded with school prospectus, having to make nail-biting decisions.

Take time to step back for a minute, read the section 'What are you looking for?' on page 97 and then decide with your child from there.

4 **When attending school open events, go beyond the 'tourist route'.** Usually the first time you venture back to school is as a parent at an open day and your brain suddenly transports you back into 'kid mode'; you find yourself following the staff obediently on the 'tourist route'. Snap out of it! It's time to ask important questions for you and your child.

Read the 'Looking at schools' checklist on page 101 to help you focus and get in the right frame of mind before you set off.

5 **Make prospective school visits count: know what to ask and where to look.** More often than not, today's parents and children are leading busy lives. You may not have time to prepare in full for the first look at a school, but rest easy, I've done the preparation for you.

Follow tips 1–10 in 'How to find out everything you need to know on school open days' on pages 99–101. Do this and you and your child will get out of any prospective school visit all you ever wanted to know. Happy hunting!

**10** Your child is brilliant
Journey's end, journey's beginning

**9** Living and learning
Making every day count!

**8** Brilliant work space
Where brain training and focus meet

**7** Goal setting and achieving
Teaching your child how to succeed

# 6 Working with schools
## Cultivating the foundation for your child's future

**5** Getting the best out of schools
What to look for beyond the 'tourist route'

**4** Cutting tests down to size
What every parent should know

**3** How your child learns best
Different ways of learning

**2** Discovering your child's gifts
Uncovering hidden treasures

**1** Inside your child's brain
Understanding the technology

# 6

Education is a partnership between parents, teachers, schools and children. Cultivating good understanding across this partnership is the key to children getting the best out of their school years. Most of the time this is exactly what happens and we all move forwards smoothly. But some of the time, humans being humans, things happen that can upset that steady flow. In this chapter, I want to share with you a number of tried and tested dodges that work because they are founded on two important truths in life. First, communication is everything when dealing with people. Second, to get the best out of each other we all like to feel valued. Remember those two things when dealing and working with schools and everyone is on to a winner when it comes to sorting out problems when they might occur and finding solutions. They incur the least effort and stress and the maximum effectiveness.

Communication is what we do every day and we hardly think about it. But it is a complicated process and from time to time we can get messages mixed up. If you have ever played Chinese whispers, you can easily see how communication can get scrambled. The message 'Send reinforcements, we are going to advance', becomes ever so quickly, 'Send six and four pence, we are going to a dance'!

Communication between home and school can sometimes be prone to mishaps like this, which are often innocently created. Wherever there are large groups of people, communication can easily go awry. Most of the time things go along swimmingly, but if something does go wrong and it involves your child, as may happen at some point given the length of time children are at school, then here is my advice. Stay calm and listen to everyone's point of view. This does not mean you are deserting your child or being passive. It means that you are sorting out what has happened and, in the process, showing yourself to be a master of diplomacy. Machiavelli would have been proud of you! None of his princes could have done it better.

# On **tanks** and **swans**

Tanks are noisy. You can see and hear them coming a mile off. Sure they pack some explosives, but you have time to bunker in. Tanks give the person they are trundling towards plenty of time to get their defences together and probably throw in some extra reinforcements for good measure. By the time tanks arrive at their destination, word has got round they are coming and that they are not happy. Hence, whoever they are coming to see have either buried their heads in the sand or can't string two words together out of nerves – or both.

My advice in dealing with schools is, don't be a tank. I know that when Billy Bad Lad poured blue dye over your child's beautiful hair you saw not blue but red and the music from *Psycho* shrieked across your mind momentarily, but swans will always win over a tank. Swans glide and appear unexpectedly; the silent attack. No one has time to prepare, bunker in or build an elaborate defence. And that means no one has time to get overly excited either. Everyone starts talking sense.

★ No one likes to argue or upset a swan because they are so very nice to deal with.

★ No one can walk over a swan because swans can get nasty and no one wants to see that, not when they were so calm and pleasant a moment ago.

This is what I call the 'paradise lost' dodge. Schools are places where calm and tranquillity are respected and hard fought for most of the time. So for a school to know they have had that excellent relationship with you and lost it is much worse than them having to face the onslaught of the 'tank'. So, basically, swans stand a better chance than a tank all around. It is also much better for everyone's blood pressure.

When it comes to committees, fêtes, sports days, charity events and other such opportunities that present themselves for parents to have a bigger say in the life of the school, it has to be said that tanks rarely get invited because they frighten everyone too much; whereas swans regularly feature in such events. Of course, that is not to say that many a tank has not successfully assumed the guise of a swan and done very well on a number of school committees. Where there is a will, there is always a way.

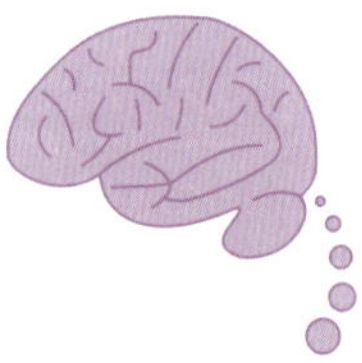

**Brilliant fact!**
Remember that schools are busy organizations. The way you approach them will determine what you get out of them. Being a 'swan' wins friends and influences people, gaining you extra points in the long-run.

## REMEMBER YOUR FOCUS

Bearing tanks and swans in mind as you walk or canter up the school steps to sort out 'the problem', remember what you are actually there to do: to find a positive mutual resolution so that your child can be successful and move on with ease. No matter how many times you envisaged it on the journey in, this resolution may not therefore fit with your visualization of justice, which involved Billy Bad Lad, who caused the problem in the first place as far as you can see, being dropped headfirst into a vat of cold custard. And you looking on smiling gleefully like the Cheshire Cat out of *Alice in Wonderland*.

Anger makes fools of us all. So when and if things go wrong, it is easy to forget your focus. This is especially the case where perhaps you don't feel that you always see eye to eye with the school your child attends. All jest aside, it is important that you get a few techniques down to help you cope and get the best out of any tense and difficult situation for you and your child, so take a look at the 'Take a moment and you may save hours' box, right.

At no point here am I suggesting that you become a 'yes' person to appease schools in difficult situations that may arise. Rather the message here is that, as with any difficult situation, a cool head is preferable to a hot head and gets the job done just as well – and that goes for children as well. Use 'What happened today at school?', overleaf, to help your child calm down and get to the facts.

## WHAT TO DO IF A PROBLEM PERSISTS

Most of the time, any problems that occur at school are usually minor, infrequent and sorted out quickly and efficiently by all concerned. Everyone moves on. However, if you find that having followed all the steps to the right and you've done everything to give a school time to work things out, and yet matters remain unresolved then, of course, you need to take a different tack. In such cases, again my advice is to think and not move in haste. Consider carefully the best route to take for your child's wellbeing.

★ Ask yourself if there really is no other avenue you could pursue that would produce the result you want amicably.

★ Brainstorm the issue with both relatives and friends.

## Take a moment and you may save hours

Before any meeting you are attending to sort out a problem, take a moment to work through these mental steps. They will help you to focus on what is really important and ensure that you are calm and in control throughout.

**STEP 1**
Pause, take a deep breath.

**STEP 2**
Clear your head.

**STEP 3**
Think about what your focus is: sorting the problem out fairly.

**STEP 4**
Remember to think about things for your child in the long term as well as the short term.

**STEP 5**
Listen to everyone's viewpoint, including that of your child.

**STEP 6**
Take stock of the actual facts.

**STEP 7**
Take time out to reflect and consider everything.

Do this and you will be best positioned to make the right decision and discuss the most beneficial outcome to the situation at your school. Everyone wins.

If, despite all this and your continued best efforts at diplomacy, you are getting no joy, you need to move beyond the people you are dealing with and find others that will listen and are in a position to act to sort out the situation professionally.

## KEEP A DIARY

In some cases, and I have only come across such situations very rarely in schools, it is important that you start keeping a diary of events. This is useful because it helps you form a practical and consistent record of what happened, with key dates to refer back to in future meetings that may then occur to sort out the problem.

It is also a good idea to back track and write down all the steps you took to show that you were acting in good faith and good will, trying to sort out the problem before you were left with no option but to take it further.

This last point is important because where a person has tried to deal calmly and rationally with the problem, and has only moved to the last resort because it was the only option left, it immediately sets the tone that you were not looking for a conflict, but have nevertheless found yourself in one. In other words, it shows that you are not the problem, rather it is the way that it has been handled that is.

## What happened today at school?

Life is life, and whether we are adults or children, we all have our good and bad days. On a good day, your child comes skipping in all full of joy. On a bad day … well, your child won't be so happy. Children can sometimes find it hard to figure out what went wrong or even how it happened. The following technique works for children and adults alike because it helps deal with problems and move on confidently.

**The golden rules of practical problem solving**

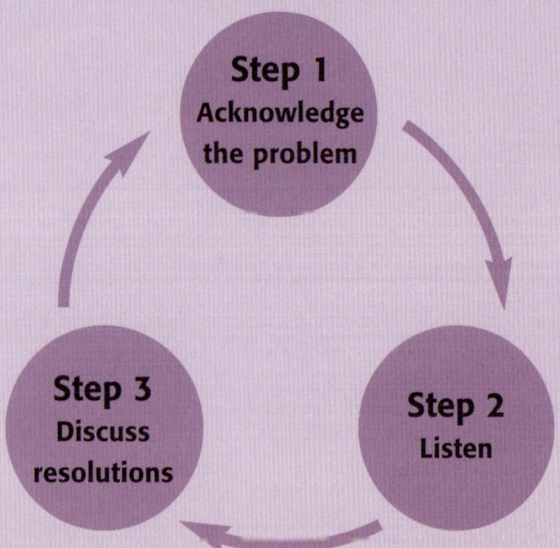


**STEP 1:** If your child has had a bad day or has a problem, **ACKNOWLEDGE** it. Humans like to be acknowledged when they have a problem. It immediately starts to make them feel better.

**STEP 2:** Let your child tell you the problem. **LISTEN**. You might listen to the problem several times over. Bite your tongue and keep listening. Humans like being heard. Listening works.

**STEP 3: DISCUSS RESOLUTIONS**. This works best when children discuss with their parents what they think they should do next. Don't make any suggestions, just discuss ideas with your child. Before children feel comfortable enough to move on, they need a plan.

The objective is to reach the point where your child feels good and can move forward confidently with a resolution in hand. To achieve this, you may work through the steps a few times. This is perfectly normal; it is how the human mind works. Your child's mind here is a bit like a computer caught in a loop. It has to decide what to do with the file before it can store it. Working through these steps ensures your child has worked through a problem, dealt with it and can now move on successfully.

# Inside your child's school

Remember that just like your bank and hospital, schools are organizations. And while every school has its own distinctive way of doing things, wherever you are in the world schools share some basic organizational structure. This is worth knowing about so that you can decide on who it may be best to set up a meeting with, depending on the nature of your concern. The basic school organizational chart below is designed to help you do this. The number of staff and departments may differ from school to school, but the basic structure will remain the same.

### A who's who in a school

**Principal**

Responsibilities include: managing school budget, making links with organizations outside of school that might benefit the children, managing staff, teaching classes

↓

**Senior management and department heads**

Responsibilities include: combining teaching classes with managing budgets and staff in their subject areas, pastoral as well as academic welfare of students in their departments and classes

↓

**Specialist teachers**

Examples are coordinators for gifted and talented children and children with special educational needs
Responsibilities include: liaising within and between senior management and department heads and teachers to ensure information is shared and applied, teaching classes

↓

**Teachers**

Responsibilities include: delivering the curriculum, ensuring academic and social welfare of children in each of the classes they teach

**TIP 1**
There is one thing common to every level – all members of staff are actively teaching classes every day. Many a parent has come to me disappointed that they turned up at their child's school to discuss a matter and didn't get to see who they wanted. Nine times out of ten this is because even though the person wanted to see the parent, they couldn't because doing so would have meant leaving 30 children unattended – and that is not an option for a teaching professional. They could end up returning to find the children climbing up the walls!

**TIP 2**
As your child's teacher is responsible for both academic and pastoral care, that person is your first port of call should you wish to talk about anything. In other words, you don't always need to feel you have to see the principal.

**TIP 3**
It is worth finding out your child's school's organizational structure and who is responsible for what at the beginning of term. In that way, should you ever need to speak to someone, you know exactly who to contact, and that saves time all around.

# Cultivate a **good relationship** with the **school**

In my experience, most of the time, most of the parents and children I work with have a good and positive working relationship with their schools and teachers. If you haven't done so already, start cultivating that relationship and making it the very best it can be. This doesn't mean sucking up to schools and teachers who can spot that kind of thing at 200 miles, it means avoiding like the plague any 'them and us'-type ideas that might make great film scripts and headlines, but belong firmly in the drama stakes.

When it comes to the school-parent relationship, the 'them and us' mentality is a nonsense that ignores the fact that the success of our children depends in the end on parents and schools working together to forge good working relationships. Such relationships have huge spin-offs for children in terms of their:

- ★ Performance across the board
- ★ Overall wellbeing
- ★ Attitude and motivation
- ★ Enhanced exchange of information, which can only help children succeed better, faster.

We live in a cynical world, where a person is quickly criticized when something goes wrong, but praise is not always as quick (or, indeed, even forthcoming) when someone gets it right. This attitude is apparent every day in the work place. Only in Hollywood films does it seem the opposite happens more frequently, which is why it can feel good to watch them.

At the end of the day, everyone likes to be appreciated for what they do and I think we therefore need more celebration of 'the wins' in life. To give you an example of how not to celebrate a win, I give you an early morning radio news item that managed to turn some positive and excellent news into a negative one for parents as they drove into work that day.

**Brilliant fact!**

Cynicism is infectious; you and your child don't need it. Break the mould. Don't just leave it to when you have the next parents' evening, or your child needs a visit to the dentist, or a problem arises, to make school contact. If you find that your child has really enjoyed a certain lesson or topic, because of how it was taught, take a minute to put pen to paper and send a little note to convey how great you think that is.

Obviously don't do this every two minutes otherwise both its currency, motives and genuineness will be questioned and the opportunity lost. But every once in a while, a genuine note to say something positive where a pat on the back is due is good. It seizes the opportunity to cultivate a relationship that sets up a positive cycle of mutual respect for parents, teachers and children alike.

> *The actual news was based on a finding that nine out of ten schools were succeeding in doing well in inspections. However, the way in which it was worded and broadcast turned it into a negative message for parents, by saying: one in ten schools are still failing inspections. Let's just take this statistic and put it in another context – nine in ten fish trawlers come back with full nets or one in ten boats don't get a full catch. It is true, of course, that it would be better if all the boats came in with a full catch, but when the majority are getting a full catch on a consistent basis, is that something to get depressed about or celebrate?*

When teachers get it right, they deserve our praise. They are with our children 75 per cent of the week and how we and our children relate to them matters at the grass roots of the teacher-parent relationship. If someone feels valued, they perform better. I bet you can remember the last time someone said a nice thing about what you did at work. It might have been a long time ago, it might have been recently, but a person can live off a positive comment for weeks!

It is easy in the mad rush at the end of the holidays and the beginning of new school terms, tests and trips to forget that what your child is doing today has a knock-on effect in the years ahead. Every once in a while, just glance over the checklist, right, to remind yourself that you and your child aren't on a sprint but a marathon, taking little steps along the way.

As a last but very important word, help your child move forward confidently at school by remembering always to celebrate the wins, no matter how big, no matter how small. Just like you and me and their teachers, children are people and love being appreciated for their efforts and gifts.

### Brilliant fact!

Remember that school is not just about academic success, but also about the social and emotional wellbeing of your child, which go hand in hand. When you are chatting to your child, also find out if they are happy generally, again nipping any problems in the bud as they occur.

## **Helping your child get the most out of school years** checklist

✓ Take each step at a time, ensuring that your child is confident in what has been learned so far.

✓ Where your child is not confident, find out why, discuss it with the relevant teachers and resolve the issue.

✓ Don't let any little problems build into big ones when, if you had only known earlier, both you and your child's teacher could have sorted it out.

✓ A classic example of a problem occurring can be when, for a quite innocent reason, a child misses a topic due to a dental appointment or being ill on that particular day. A blip then occurs because a key piece of knowledge is missing for the homework.

✓ To prevent this happening, have an informal chat with your child each week to make sure they feel on top of everything.

✓ Have a peek together at the homework book, too. In that way, you can see what is happening as it is happening, pinpoint any problems, share successes, and help your child to move on successfully.

✓ Remember that education is a partnership. When schools, parents and children work together, everyone wins and children succeed.

# The **route** to **success** 6

In this chapter you have learned that knowing how to deal effectively with schools can save you time and energy through life's inevitable ups and downs. Cultivating good communication and a positive working relationship with your child's school is the cornerstone to ensuring children get the most from their teachers and school years. Your child can look forward to plenty of years of success ahead.

1 **Always be a 'swan' and never be 'tank' when dealing with schools.** Anger makes fools of us all. As you approach your child's school take a moment. Think! What is your real focus? Blowing your top or getting a problem resolved? If you are thinking straight it will be the latter objective that guides what you do next.

If you find yourself in a situation like this, follow the steps in 'Take a moment and you may save hours' on page 107.

2 **Remember that school years are about social as well as academic wellbeing.** Each week have a gentle and supportive chat with your child to find out how things are going on at every level at school.

Use the checklist 'Helping your child get the most out of school years' on page 111 to nip any problems gently and quickly in the bud.

3 **If your child tells you about a problem, acknowledge it and listen.** Most of the time children will have great days at school, but there may be times when things go wrong. This is normal. What isn't always easy to do is just listen to children when they have just come home from school and are telling you what happened at high speed.

To help calm children down after a not-so-good day at school, follow the cycle on the chart on page 108. It is simple and effective and when you have done it you will know what to do next.

4 **Know who to speak to when in school, to always get the best result.** If you went into your local bank about a specific matter, you would know who you needed to speak to and why. You would also approach your bank as an organization with rules and regulations to follow. Approaching your child's school is no different in this respect because it is an organization too.

Use the guide 'Inside your child's school' on page 109 to find out who you need to speak to in advance. Whatever the situation, good or bad, you know who to contact to get the best result.

5 **Remember education is a partnership, cultivate that and everyone wins.** Set up a cycle of positive communication between you and the school by not waiting until things go wrong to make contact. Instead, when things are going right, take the opportunity to praise people.

Look at the Brilliant fact! on page 110. Don't be afraid to make contact first with a positive note or visit. It so easy to do and sets up a great foundation from which to move forward.

# 7 Goal setting and achieving

## Teaching your child how to succeed

# 7

For the children of past generations, when it came to deciding their future, tradition more than individual choice held sway. More often than not, children followed their parents' footsteps, occasionally having the opportunity to break the mould and do something different. Following the massive social and economic changes of the past three decades, the reverse may now be true. Traditional jobs and career paths have been forced to make way for the rapid change that comes with an increasingly global knowledge economy.

In this century, traditional routes in education that divided students into university graduates and those who chose to train in practical skills have become blurred. Careers today demand that people are flexible enough to have a range of skills and qualifications. No matter what the field, learning is not a one-stop but lifelong affair. Educational options available worldwide have burgeoned to accommodate this change in how we live and learn. The choice on offer is huge for young people to consider. None of us can second guess the future. But what we can do is help our children prepare to make the best choices they can by learning how to develop their own gifts and talents.

The challenge for today's children, therefore, is not a lack of choice, but how to maximize upon it. However, the broader the range of opportunities on offer, the more questions arise about which route is best for your child. When parents come to me, this is the concern that underpins their questions: what should I be doing to help my child make the right choices? How do I ensure they make the best of their gifts and carve out a successful and rewarding future?

Helping you and your child work through these important questions and find a route that works for your child is what this chapter is all about. Indeed, helping parents and children answer these important questions and make right choices for their future is what lies at the heart of the *Make your Child Brilliant* journey. Everything you and your child have learned up to now has prepared you for this chapter. And now you are ready to make the most of it!

# The foundations of brilliance

Before you and your child start thinking about dreams and goals, there are three rules to guide you towards success. They comprise the key beliefs that are the core of my philosophy.

## RULE 1

**There is no one or 'right way to success'; only the way that suits you and your child**

It is not a new observation that what works for some people doesn't work for others. That is just the way it is. What worked for you may not work for your child because, first, you are living in a different age and environment and, second, your child is, of course, a unique individual. As with everything you have learned so far here, that fact has to be the natural starting point in any journey your child is going to undertake to realize their own gifts.

## RULE 2

**There is no 'perfect' mould to aspire to, there is only the individual child and they are perfect enough**

I know it may seem an obvious thing to say, but no one is perfect. And yet over the last few decades we human beings seem to have got ourselves in a pickle over the idea of 'perfection': media images can imply that we are too fat, too tall, too thin or too small. The *Make your Child Brilliant* journey doesn't have 'too's, it just has 'ones' – individual children with their own unique gifts and personalities, which are there to be celebrated, supported, loved and valued.

I would like to know something: just who was it anyway that decided that all of us and our children had to measure up to some 'perfect ideal'? I'd like to know because whoever they were has caused us a lot of unnecessary problems and scared us witless along the way. Our children must do such a thing at such an age, or else; our children must score such a thing on such a test, or else. Funnily enough, look at the history of people that are brilliant in any field and more often than not their journey there was less than perfect. The fighter pilot that suffered the loss of his legs, and was told he would never fly again, only to prove them all wrong. The self-taught artist that developed her own style and so wowed a nation of critics. The sailor that was told not to sail off the 'edge of the map', only to find that he did and there were some people over the other side. There is no limit to the human spirit. Every mould you can think of and the human spirit will always break it.

I once saw a *Star Trek* episode. Captain Kirk had landed on a planet where there only ever seemed to be two people that he came across, one dark-haired man and one blonde-haired woman. Eventually it transpired that due to some terrible disaster, everyone on the planet had ended up looking exactly the same; it was driving the inhabitants mad and that is why they had put out the distress signal.

Diversity is good, and in an era when children have so much to choose from, it is time to celebrate that more than perhaps is particularly obvious from the media at present. As we work in this chapter together, you will see a great deal of emphasis upon recognizing and celebrating diversity in our children's individual gifts and moving onward and upward from there.

### RULE 3

**We decide our own limits; we do not let others set them for us**

When we are first born and discover the world around us, we feel we can fly, reach the sky. We can do anything and nothing is going to stop us. It is a great feeling. Then we meet obstacles and competitors, people who like us, others who do not and the game of life is on. The game is, of course, a serious matter because there are various pressures that come into play to knock our self-confidence and our belief in ourselves the minute we can walk and talk. People may decide they have the right to place limits on our ability and what they believe we can achieve. Get into the habit of listening to such people and children are never going to realize that the only person who can decide their dreams and what they can achieve is themselves.

There is an old African proverb that says: a wise man sorts out his own problems. The truth is that each of us is best placed to be able to make our own choices and set our own course. With the knowledge you and your child have gained so far, you too are in a position to make an informed choice.

Following the steps overleaf, you and your child can learn together how to harness all that you have been given in terms of your individual gifts and not just dream about your future, but actually begin to make it happen, right now, today.

## What you programme the brain with really matters

Research tries to understand the brilliance of the human brain as a computer, but it is acknowledged that any computer modelling can only ever be a highly simplified replication of the complex organ that is the human brain. However, much as we can programme a computer, the brain is also receptive to being programmed.

★ What you put into the brain affects what you get out of it. For children this is an important fact to remember, particularly as they develop friendship groups and start to think about their future. It is beneficial for your child to have positive friends who support their dreams and ambitions. In that way, your child's brain receives positive feedback and an upward spiral of 'can do' thought emerges.

★ Explain this to your child and you will better enable them to make judgements as to who to try to avoid and who to hang out with in order to have a great time and win all round.

# The art and science **of goal setting**

## STEP 1

### Decide upon a goal

At this point, both you and your child need to be sitting down together with a notebook and pen, because your child's journey to realizing dreams starts here. Goals don't work for people unless they comprise their own dreams and ambitions and are borne out of their individual gifts and talents. In the work place and at our leisure we have all come across the accountant who really wanted to be a professional footballer and spends every living hour wishing he had done that, or the golf professional that wanted to be a heart surgeon and is bored witless and burnt out by coaching in his mid forties.

Whoever set them on the course that became the life they didn't want to have probably did so with love and good will, but that doesn't change the fact that the goal was set without really looking at the full range of gifts and talents and passions of the child first. If you or someone you discuss this fact with is not yet convinced, let me share with you the story of Francis.

> *Even when he was young, Francis loved anything and everything to do with organizing and working with other people. Charity work and business fascinated him. He loved the hustle and bustle of making things happen and working in teams. His father, however, had other ideas; he decided that a one-way ticket to success for Francis was medical school. There was just one problem with this: Francis couldn't stand the sight of blood. But that didn't deter his father. Francis gritted his teeth and completed his medical degree for his father. Immediately on graduation day Francis handed over the degree certificate to his father, with the words, "Here is your dream, now I am off to find mine." Francis found a job in a retail store while he studied for an MBA. He then went on to run not just one but several successful businesses worldwide, as well as help develop an international children's charity. Needless to say, he made certain he didn't make the same mistake with his children. They are doing just fine – pursuing their own dreams.*

The key to successful goal setting is to work from the foundation of knowing what your individual gifts and strengths are. You and your child will now have a good idea of where their individual strengths and abilities lie from the work you both did together in Chapter 2. Take a moment now to remind yourselves of these. Once you have done that, you are ready to begin discussing together short- and long-term goals with your child.

Practice makes perfect with goal setting. Starting with the defining and achieving little goals first helps children get practice in setting and working towards the big goals in their life. But the real trick to achieving any goal is to know how to actually set a goal. Often children think they know what a goal is, but more often than not they don't. Making sure children understand what a goal actually is, is one of the cornerstones of the *Make your Child Brilliant* journey.

For example, a vague goal, like 'I want to be famous', 'rich' or a 'celebrity' is not a goal at all; it is a woolly idea, because unless you break it down, it doesn't actually mean anything, and yet these are things we can often hear children say are their goals.

Real goal setting, to be effective, is like mentally sharpening a spear into a fine and solid tip. Children need to break down what it is, for example, about being 'rich' or being 'famous' that is attractive in their initial goal offering. This will probably reveal a number of factors that have influenced their choice and eventually they will arrive at what they really want to be or do.

Other children may be more direct: 'I want to be a vet'. That is fine, but either way they need to find out what it is about that particular goal that is attractive to them. In that way, they will be able to find out the real essence of their goal, and what they therefore really want to do.

When you talk through goals with your child, don't rush it and, whatever you do, remember that gentle support and no pushing always yield the best results.

## Break down goals into long term and short term

Once you have refined the long-term goal, work on it together to define it and make its description as detailed as possible. Use a notebook to jot down the goal and refine it as much as you can. Refining a goal by thinking about its details is important. Imagine you set off to redecorate your house, it would never happen if you did not fill out precisely the detail of what that meant: which colours in which rooms and why. It is the same with any kind of goal, to make it materialize you have to fill in the detail. For example, say your child's goal is to be a veterinary surgeon, find out: has your child realized they will need to excel in science? Where will your child work, locally or in a city? If the goal is to be a writer or journalist, find out what kind of writer? What kinds of things interest your child: news items, history, live theatre, television, sport, film, or a mixture of these?

Remember that there are no right and wrong answers here, only a detailed goal. All of this discussion and mentally filling in the fine detail helps your child's mind to sharpen the goal. Working in this way helps children find out what they really want for themselves. It gives them a tangible goal, as opposed to some vague and woolly idea. Making their goal tangible in their mind is really important in goal setting. If an idea isn't thought through, the brain cannot work towards it because it doesn't exist, it isn't real. But with something tangible, the brain can work towards it effectively because it is very real.

Now that your child has sorted out the long-term goal, you are ready to look at the short-term goals. Short-term goals are just as important as a child's big goal, they are the little pegs that enable children to climb up and reach towards the bigger goal. Little does not mean less important; these goals are the ones that enable children to find out how empowering it feels to set themself an objective and achieve it. It also gently shows children the art of overcoming obstacles to achieve what they want in life. All of us are born with a range of gifts and talents, and that means that we also have areas we need to work on to produce an end result. For example, maybe we are fantastic at

**Brilliant fact!**
Two reasons why people don't achieve goals: first, they don't really believe in the goal, because it is not their goal, it is someone else's. Second, they don't make the goal precise and specific enough for it to be something that the human mind can visualize and thus work towards. Where children learn the art of setting goals for themselves early they are onto a winner straightaway.

**Brilliant fact!**
Whatever your child says their goal is, remember to keep bringing them back to the fact that in order to succeed they need to value their own strengths, their own gifts and set a goal from there.

computer science, but need to work on learning and mastering better drawing skills to become a computer animator. We could be a very imaginative writer, but need to sharpen up our punctuation so we can communicate ideas clearer. Even Einstein is reputed to have said that he could have done with sharpening up his maths skills to help him with his physics problems!

As we established at the beginning of this chapter, no one is perfect but that is OKAY. It is what makes us human, of course. Whenever I am working with children, the sooner they realize this, the happier they become and begin to be much more honest and open about the areas they need to work on. When that happens, an upward spiral of achievement begins. They start to have altogether much more confidence in tackling any areas they feel they need to. This is because when working towards a bigger goal, they can see their smaller goals in perspective. They have real focus and see more clearly what it is that they have to do to achieve their dream; and one of those is having short-term goals to get the job done.

So now take a few minutes with your child to celebrate the fact that you are both human and that your child has fantastic gifts and abilities, but just like Einstein, there are other areas that need to be worked on, too, to achieve the long-term goal. One of the things I find works well in my workshops on this topic is to share with children how much I wanted to do the work I do, which involves a lot of presenting. I tell them the story of when I had to first present something in front of children and how nervous I was. All I had to do was two minutes, but to me it felt like two weeks! Today I have presented my work in front of thousands of people, and have no fear at all. How did I do it?

First, I acknowledged the problem and tackled it head on. I looked at the things I could do better and knocked them over one by one with practice and persistence. Together with your child, work through the following:

★ Acknowledge and chat honestly about any obstacles or areas that need to be worked on.

★ Make it real. Celebrate the fact that overcoming obstacles is what makes us human; share with your child an example of how you too had to overcome an obstacle to achieve a goal.

★ Do a real troubleshoot, no holds barred, get it all out – where does your child see the biggest obstacles? Make a list together of all of these.

★ Prioritize: which is the most important one to tackle immediately?

★ Break down the obstacle. What are the short-term goals you could put in place to knock over the obstacle?

★ Make a list of short-term goals; these should have a simple objective and a precise timescale. For example: 'This week ask more questions about homework and projects so that I can get better marks'.

★ Now your child is ready to fill in 'Goal Peak Mountain', opposite.

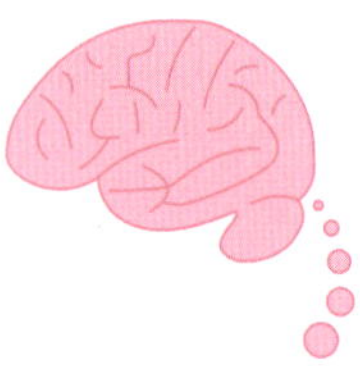

## Brilliant fact!

Making a goal tangible does not mean stopping short of reaching for the moon; it means making it more possible for children to achieve it, by showing them how to make their goal real. Children should never feel afraid to reach for the moon. Reach for the moon and you are always going to land on a star. Don't reach at all and what could have, should have, might have been, will always be there nagging at the back of your mind. How silly is that? So go for it – always.

Name: ..............................................................................................................

# Goal Peak Mountain

Using a pencil, let your child fill in first 'My big goal' in the space at the top of the mountain. Then, starting from the bottom, your child can write a short-term goal at each of the 'pegs' to show what needs to be tackled to get to the top of the peak. Doing this in pencil means that once one obstacle has been tackled and overcome, that particular short-term goal can be rubbed out and replaced with another, as and when your child needs to. Alternatively, your child can draw a Goal Peak Mountain onto a piece of paper, fill it in as appropriate and pin it to a notice board or wall. This acts as a focal point for children, reminding them where they are going and especially how they are going to get there.

**My big goal:**------------------------------------

**Timescale:**------------------------------------

**Short-term goal:**------------------------------

**Timescale:**------------------------------------

**Short-term goal:**------------------------------

**Timescale:**------------------------------------

**Short-term goal:**------------------------------

**Timescale:**------------------------------------

## STEP 2

**Use visualization: seeing is believing for the human brain**

What the mind sees it believes. Visualization may be a relatively new word to some, but human beings have been practising it for years. Cave paintings, wrought in great detail and colour, show that successful hunting scenes were painted on walls where everyone could see them. For those uninitiated in hunting, this spelt out a reassuring visual fact. When they went hunting despite all the dangers that lay ahead, they too could be successful; after all they had 'seen it with their own eyes'. When successful sports people set out to win a game, they visualize it and then make it happen. This is as true today as it ever was. Some things change, but not everything. The same effect can be used to help children achieve their goals.

I have used visualization techniques to help children achieve their goals for over two decades. It is really simple to do. Both you and your child can do this, following the technique described below.

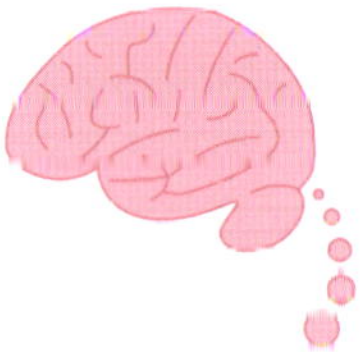

**Brilliant fact!**

The human brain believes what it sees. If it sees a picture in its mind's eye, that shows you achieving a goal – and that picture is sufficiently wrought with detail and colour – the mind believes it to be real.

### The power of visualization

In brain terms what is happening is that the mind has seen something and now it believes it. So it starts to work in a positive way, making the goal possible. It is re-programming the mind to think in a different way about what is and is not achievable. Now that it has 'seen' that your goal is achievable, it starts acting that way and the effect of this is that instead of looking for barriers to your success, the brain starts thinking about ways to make it happen instead.

Visualization is a tool that further develops hopes and desires that we aim towards. It is said that before Einstein wrote up his theories he visualized them. This may seem ingenious, but if you have ever planned to go on holiday but have been

## Using DIY visualization technique

Sit down in a comfortable chair with your arms relaxed and breathing regularly.

★ Close your eyes and see within your mind a clear, white canvas. Imagine the day you have achieved your goal.

★ Begin to paint onto the canvas a mental picture of this day, filling in every detail you can think of:

– What you are wearing and where it is taking place
– The colours that surround you
– The sounds, the smells, the atmosphere, people congratulating you
– How proud you feel; how great you feel inside.

★ Fill in the whole scene until it is a vibrant, living picture in your mind. Hold that picture for a short time; this is your moment of glory.

★ Now imagine you have a camera and you are going to take a snapshot of the big day. Get the picture you have painted in your mind really clear; the colours vibrant. Take the picture and hold that picture. Then slowly open your eyes.

held back by the thought of the price tag that goes with it, you may have found yourself using visualization without knowing it to convince yourself to get your chequebook out. Ever visualized yourself sitting on the beach at the destination of your choice, and later made that all-important booking?

Visualization can be a real mental tool to programming yourself to achieve the goals you want to achieve. Now that your child has learned what a goal is and how to achieve it, you can make full use of this visualization technique. In my work I like to take children to a place that might represent what it is that they want to achieve. I then take a snapshot of them there to stick on their bedroom wall, so that any time they doubt themselves there is the visual reminder that it IS possible.

Another way to do this is for children to find cuttings from magazines that represent where they want to be and then make a collage of the pictures and stick a photograph of themselves right in the middle. They can then put it on their bedroom wall or notice board as a reminder of their focus and goals.

## STEP 3

**Use what works best for you to learn**

In Chapter 3 you and your child found that 'one size doesn't fit all' in the ways that people learn. You and your child found out:

★ How to experiment with different ways of approaching learning.

★ How to find out the best ways to learn.

★ What makes learning more fun and easy.

★ How to take ownership of learning to be more effective with this skill.

All of this is important as children work to overcome obstacles and build on their strengths to achieve their goals. Knowing

## Troubleshooting obstacles together

If you discover that your child is finding a subject or topic particularly hard, as always, tackle the worst first: find out where exactly the problem lies and work from there.

★ If it is a problem in class that is worrying your child, make an appointment with the class teacher and/or school and gently nip it in the bud so that it remains a short-term as opposed to a long-term problem.

★ If it is a problem elsewhere, work the problem through with your child, and together you will come up with a logical and effective course of action to remedy any situation.

The main objective is that your child should always be left feeling in the driving seat, actively involved in helping to map out and achieve their short- and long-term goals. Keep that in mind always and you and your child will succeed.

what was learned in Chapter 3 means that children are now equipped with a range of techniques for learning. Any areas that need attention to overcome their short-term goals can more readily be tackled. They can also maximize upon their gifts to achieve their long-term goals.

If it has been some time since you last visited Chapter 3 – How your child learns best – now is a good time to revise what you learned there so that your child is ready to move on to the next step.

### STEP 4

**Celebrate the wins as self-directed learners**

Your child has learned how to set and achieve a goal. Now your child needs to learn an equally important step – how to celebrate wins as a self-directed learner. Self-directed learning is what makes any person excel in any field. This occurs when people get into the habit of taking responsibility for setting and achieving their own goals – and then rewarding themselves when they achieve success.

## The secret of brilliance: the art of self-rewarding

The reward in itself is unimportant. This is because the reward in the end is no longer a material object but a more precious thing: it is the personal sense of self-worth and self-confidence a child gets from taking charge of learning to reach future goals. Children can train their brains to do this and get that great personal satisfaction. All that is needed to get them started are some simple sticky stars and a list of short-term goals. Using 'Your child's star self-reward system', overleaf, children can fill in the short-term goals that they are working upon. Remember that it is these short-term goals and achieving them that will, in the end, combine to enable children to make their dreams come true. And that with each of these small steps they are helping themselves achieve their big, long-term goal.

Once children have the art of setting their own short-term goals and rewarding themselves accordingly, their brains have learned something that will empower them for life. They will have learned that they hold their destiny in their own hands and whatever they really set their mind to, they can achieve. The real beauty of it is this:

★ When children learn to set high standards naturally for themselves, they build confidence in their own abilities.

★ With confidence comes the motivation to do and achieve more.

This cycle of thought always works better than imposed goals and standards – because as human beings we take pleasure in achieving our own goals in our own individual way. Once children realize the power of this and see it working for them, they never need look back. They are training themselves to achieve their goals, and when they do that they are on a winning path.

The art of self-rewarding is crucial to achieving self-directed learning that will set a child up for life. When children self-reward, they learn how to reward themselves for hard work, to take pride in their achievements and responsibility for achieving the goals they set.

Even if at first they cheat on their self-reward system, they soon realize that cheating isn't a smart thing to do, and will then begin to self-direct themselves to work for real achievement. This process is between the child and their brain: learning how to control it to get a better result for themself.

Offering alternative rewards will only disrupt the journey to self-rewarding. Let your child get on with figuring this out and give gentle support in reaching the conclusion that being able to work responsibly with a self-reward system is the best way forward.

That doesn't mean that when children, through effort and hard work, pull off a fantastic win they can't be lavished with praise and congratulations. Celebrating wins is great. It is a positive reinforcement for all of us to continue to strive for what we want to achieve. In fact, self-rewarding is about teaching children that they have within themselves the power to achieve whatever it is that they put their mind to.

## STEP 5

**Remember that life doesn't stand still; neither does opportunity**

Keep open to new opportunities and new goals. Our lives and those of our children do not stand still, and neither do our goals. With new opportunities, children will discover new gifts and talents that open up further routes to success. Make it a habit to regularly chat together about where your child wants to go, what your child wants to do and how your child wants to get there. Remember there are at least two ways to do and achieve absolutely anything, and keep working together to map out that route to success.

## STEP 6

**Life is an undulating journey, we have ups and downs**

The trick to achieving any goal once you have set it and are happy with it, is to keep on going until you reach it. This is harder said than done, but remember that when the rain comes and you are waiting for the sunny days to come again, that they will indeed return. Persist and keep moving and the sun will be there shining on your face again. I have never come across anyone who has achieved brilliance in their field and found that every day was a sunny one. Indeed, in many cases they have overcome extraordinary difficulties by just keeping going and keeping their focus.

Any time your child has a doubt, let them just imagine that they are on that mountain on page 121. If it were a real mountain, it would be daft to climb up so far only to then go back down. Usually the point where a climb gets the hardest is right there near the summit. At that point you just have to tell your mind, keep moving forward: right leg, then left leg ... and then, before you know it, you are there.

I am a great believer in using physical exercise to sharpen up children's sense of self-belief as well as their problem-solving and thinking skills. Climbing is a very good brain and body workout, leaving you with a feel-good glow afterwards. And so if you are feeling up to it, a great mental preparation to go with the steps in this chapter is to actually take the whole family out for a good walk! I am not thinking the Matterhorn or Everest here! I am talking about a simple good old-fashioned walk, which involves reaching the top of a small hill, just so children can experience first hand that fantastic sense of self-achievement when they reach the top.

Once children have done this, their brain has, in effect, experienced a real-life mini version of what it is like to focus on something they want to do and achieving it. Do that and your child will get 100 per cent more out of this chapter than if they had not done this simple but highly effective thing. So! Go on, give it a go and feel great about yourself too. Plus the bonus point is, of course, it costs you absolutely nothing!

# Your child's star self-reward system

Take a pencil and ask your child to write down the following things in the spaces provided below and opposite.

★ Let your child set down a list of any short-term goals for this and the coming days and weeks. There are four spaces for goals on these pages, but it doesn't matter if the list is shorter or longer. It is only the goals themselves that matter.

★ For each goal, ask your child to set down a precise timescale that allows time to reach that goal.

★ After the timescale has passed, revisit the chart together and discuss how well your child thinks the goals have been achieved and what number of stars should be self-rewarded. Ask the question, 'Do you think you deserve the whole three stars, two or just one in each goal you have set yourself?' Then keep quiet and let your child be the next to utter another word – this is what I call 'the silent close'. Let your child decide.

★ When you have this chat, it should be informal, no pressure and really like a matter of fact discussion. The main thing to encourage in this discussion is openness and honesty. This technique is about children reflecting honestly on whether or not they have really worked hard enough and achieved what they set out to achieve. If your child smiles and fools around, don't be overly stern, but with a straight face ask the question again gently and repeat the silent close. By keeping quiet and hearing what children have to say, they give you and, more importantly, themselves the honest answer and reward themselves with the relevant star count.

**GOAL 1**

My goal is:------------------------------------------------------------

My timescale for achieving this goal is:----------------------------------------

How well do I think I have achieved this goal?------------------------------------

☆ ☆ ☆

**GOAL 1**

My goal is:..........................................................................................

My timescale for achieving this goal is:...................................................

How well do I think I have achieved this goal?........................................

☆ ☆ ☆

**GOAL 1**

My goal is:..........................................................................................

My timescale for achieving this goal is:...................................................

How well do I think I have achieved this goal?........................................

☆ ☆ ☆

**GOAL 1**

My goal is:..........................................................................................

My timescale for achieving this goal is:...................................................

How well do I think I have achieved this goal?........................................

☆ ☆ ☆

# The **route** to **success** 7

It is a very old saying, but a true one: if you don't know where you are going, you could end up somewhere else. In this chapter your child has learned the art and science of real goal setting. They know how to set their own goals and make them happen. Your child has now learned a very valuable skill that will help them achieve what they want, not just in school but throughout life. And that is worth its weight in gold.

1 **Let your child decide on a goal.** Children's dreams and ambitions are their own, as are their gifts. When children work from the foundations of knowing what they are good at and what they want to achieve they have a much better chance of achieving that goal because they will have the personal motivation to succeed.

Read the case study on page 118 and the Brilliant facts! on page 119 to help you think about the importance of working with children's gifts and dreams so they can set goals and start making them happen.

2 **Refine goals. The brain likes precision and detail in goals.** There is a big difference between a wish list and a goal. Typically a child might say, 'I wish I could do better in my homework'. To the brain this doesn't mean anything because you haven't told it what 'better' means. Is it getting a better and precise grade? Is it presenting your work more neatly?

Read Step 1 on pages 118–20 and the Brilliant fact! on page 120 to help your child understand how to set goals successfully.

3 **What the brain sees it believes.** Since prehistoric cave paintings, humankind has always used pictures to help spur them on to greater things. Visualization works in the same way and is great brain training.

Work through the 'Using DIY visualization technique' on page 122, which enables children to create a mental image of their goal. In turn this helps their mind have a focus and to succeed.

4 **'Keep on going', don't let anything get you down.** Ask anyone who has achieved brilliance in any given field and they all have the same story to tell: at many turns in the road they had to face and overcome obstacles – and then move on.

Whenever obstacles occur, help your child deal with and overcome them, beginning with 'Troubleshooting obstacles together' on page 123.

5 **Break down big goals into little ones and give them precise timescales.** Think of climbing a mountain and you have to build in little goals to get to where you want to go. Help children achieve their big dreams by showing them how to break down their goal into little steps, all of which they can take in their stride confidently and happily.

Visit 'Goal Peak Mountain' on page 121 to help your child set and use little goals so they can make the big goal happen.

6 **Celebrate the wins and let children reward themselves.** Always celebrate the wins. No matter how big or how small, they all count. The operative words here are 'let children reward themselves'. Real reward for achievement is all about feeling good inside, it is not about the size or cost of the prize. The prize is the achievement itself!

Go to 'Your child's star self-reward system' on pages 126–7 to help children get started on self-rewarding when they achieve their goals.

**10** Your child is brilliant
Journey's end, journey's beginning

**9** Living and learning
Making every day count!

**8 Brilliant work space**
**Where brain training and focus meet**

**7** Goal setting and achieving
Teaching your child how to succeed

**6** Working with schools
Cultivating the foundation for your child's future

**5** Getting the best out of schools
What to look for beyond the 'tourist route'

**4** Cutting tests down to size
What every parent should know

**3** How your child learns best
Different ways of learning

**2** Discovering your child's gifts
Uncovering hidden treasures

**1** Inside your child's brain
Understanding the technology

# 8

The traditional boundaries between work and home space have increasingly become blurred. Business is making more use of computers and the internet, which means that for many more parents today, 'going to work' may mean simply going to their home office or study and logging on to their email. Children are encouraged by schools to use the net for their school projects. In fact, education the world over is keen to promote computer literacy among children. More often than not, parents and children can find they both want to use their home PC or laptop to do their 'home work'. In my experience this shift for families in the use of technology in the home has lead to many parents having to rethink their children's work space. This is because while computers and technology are great things, children's work space at home can, in fact, be cluttered with hardware and unless children know how to manage it, this can be a source of distraction. The purpose of this chapter is therefore twofold:

★ Teaching children to 'manage' their technology better so that they can get the best benefits from it in their learning.

★ Getting children to rethink how their work space is organized so that they can focus and concentrate better on achieving their goals and ambitions.

This may seem a simple and obvious thing to do, but as you and your child work through this chapter you will find that it has some surprises in store for the way you work too.

In a technology driven world, while we have bought technology and put it into our homes, it hasn't exactly come with a parent manual of how to help children harness its learning benefits, without also falling captive to its distractions. The techniques I share with you and your child in this chapter let children see technology in a whole new light and with that realization they can learn how to manage their time and their work space more effectively.

# The **five steps** to creating an **effective work space**

## STEP 1

### Taking out a time audit

The first step in children managing new technology is for them to find out how, in fact, it is managing them and their time. When we are young, time seems less important than when we are older. Without being aware of its importance, youngsters can take it for granted, so they need something tangible for them to understand how easily distractions can rob them of precious hours.

One of the techniques I use with children is very simple. I let them become a sleuth for a week to see how they spend their time. I encourage them to be honest with themselves and let them keep a tally of how much time they clock up at the behest of their computer games console, mobile, MP3 player, DVD, TV and any other object in their 'technology portfolio'. I also ask them to keep a tally of how much time they spend on homework together with comments and results they get during that week. The result usually amounts to a very interesting and telling story.

Let your child try this out using the 'My precious time audit', opposite. Honesty is the best policy to get the best out of the time audit. Share this point and let your child feel free to fill in how much time is spent on each activity in an average day for each day of the week. The results may be amazing both for your child and for you!

This exercise may not remedy the distractions immediately, but if there is a real problem, for example like not having enough sleep worked into your child's schedule so that they can recharge their brain (!), it will certainly provide you both with the tangible sums that speak for themselves. Sums like this cannot be argued with, leaving but one sensible option: better schedule and time management.

### Creating a time plan

To help your child, aim to work out a balanced schedule together along the lines described in the 'Helping your child design a technology management schedule', opposite. I call it this because it is not really about just doing homework any more for children. In practical terms it is about managing an increasing range of technology. Do not be tempted to impose a schedule onto your child. Remember: big or small humans dislike impositions, they love collaboration. Working it out together reinforces the fact that your child has the power to take charge of learning opportunities.

# My precious time audit

Ask your child to fill in honestly how much time they spend on each activity in an average day.

| Technology | Time spent | | | | | | |
|---|---|---|---|---|---|---|---|
| | Mon | Tues | Wed | Thurs | Fri | Sat | Sun |
| Computer games | | | | | | | |
| TV | | | | | | | |
| DVD | | | | | | | |
| CDs | | | | | | | |
| MP3 player | | | | | | | |
| Robotic cars, toys | | | | | | | |
| Mobile phone | | | | | | | |
| Other | | | | | | | |
| Daily total | | | | | | | |
| Homework | | | | | | | |

TOTAL hours spent on 'My technology portfolio':

TOTAL hours spent on my homework:

Actual homework results:

# Helping your child design a technology management schedule

Remind your child to build into this schedule the reality of their own working week. In a notebook or on a piece of paper, let your child draw a column or row for each day of the week and then carefully plan for:

★ The homework time needed each evening and at weekends in order to complete assignments. Remind your child to include breaks to refresh the mind at 45-minute intervals.

★ Time in the evenings for own choice of leisure and relaxation after homework has been done.

★ Any additional after-school activities that occur in a normal week.

★ Brain recharging time: that wonderful thing called sleep!

With so much going on in our busy 21st-century lives, it may take two or three times to get this all worked out, but when your child achieves this, you will both have a better sense of what needs to be done in order to get the results you want. Remind your child not to cheat and to take into account the full realities of their working week. Keep things practical and well-balanced.

# My precious time contract

My time is precious and so I use it wisely.

I balance my time to include work, rest and play.

I don't let technology manage my time,
I manage technology.

I do my homework first so it doesn't hang over me.

When I finish my homework I play and relax.

I need my rest, so I know when it is time
to go to bed.

I don't need Mum or Dad to tell me because
that is for babies!

I do it myself because I am brilliant!

I AM
BRILLIANT

Signed ______________________

Date ________________________

Once complete, your child can put the time audit and the schedule somewhere personal, such as on a bedroom wall or notice board. The purpose is twofold:

★ To act as a visual reminder of how much time was being wasted.
★ To help reinforce the fact that your child has the power to manage time more effectively to get better results.

To complete the exercise, read 'My precious time contract', opposite, together. Let your child read it and sign it at the bottom. Make a copy and your child can pin it next to the other two. This affirmation is a very strong and effective technique.

Where I have used it with children it has made them think about time and how they can start to manage it more effectively. Learning how to take charge of and manage their time and distractions better enables them to achieve their goals.

## STEP 2

### Space and thought association: getting into the habit of homework

Human beings are creatures of habit. We can learn good or bad habits, but either way they stay with us. Habits have strong connections to place and space. Think about if you or someone you knew ever smoked, nine times out of ten they started it as a social habit in a social space; it was something they 'got into' whenever they were around other folk trying to relax.

Space and function go together in the human psyche and for that reason children need a special space that they can call their own to do their homework. This does not need to be an expensive affair. The emphasis is on them having a permanent space in the house that is theirs to set up for study and homework, not on how big or expensive it is. This is a subtle point, but think back to famous scholars and they may only have had a very humble space, but they made it a haven, or even a shrine for their work and ideas. Personal effects that meant something to them adorned their work space, pictures of loved ones, flowers.

Where children have a corner in their bedroom or in the house somewhere that they can call their own, they can begin to make it a shrine for learning and their own success. Within that space they can have reminders around them of why they are studying and what it is all for. A notice board above their work space can house:

★ Visual reminders of their long-term and short-term goals. For example, a picture of their ultimate goal. This would be either one they have painted or even a picture from the visualization (see page 122) or a photograph of themselves in a place associated with their goal.

★ The contract they signed with themselves to manage their time (opposite) and their self-reward system (see pages 126–7).

Having worked with children worldwide, I find that they love bright colours, and so instead of only ever using white paper, they may use coloured paper to brighten up these displays and make them their own.

Having a space to call their own for homework is the beginning of children

**Brilliant fact!**

To continue to do the same thing and expect a different result is the technical definition of insanity.

This is one of my favourite phrases whenever I am getting parents or children to focus on changing their current working pattern to create a better one. It's just one of those phrases that, once heard, children and adults can't help smiling at it because it is so true, and a great argument for change. So use it when you are supporting your child to figure out a better weekly schedule.

getting into good homework habits. It becomes a place in their mind that is associated with achieving their dreams and working to the goals they have set themselves. In other words, the term 'homework' begins to have meaning and purpose that brings rewards. Immediately a child sits in this personal space their brain is saying, 'This is my special place and I can make my dreams come true here.'

## STEP 3

### Dressing for success

How can children train their brains to start focusing and get ready for homework? The answer lies in understanding that humans have rituals. Here are two well-known rituals that produce very effective results.

**A** The first step in a football team being able to win any game is to get dressed for it. They put on their 'football kit' and their mind knows that what it is preparing to do at that moment is not to ride a bike, get married or cook a meal. It is now doing a very precise activity called football.

**B** It's Monday morning and you are off to work. You get suited and booted and wear your 'work clothes'. Chatting to mothers I often find that if they have been off on maternity leave, their whole wardrobe has changed, and going back to work they feel the need to rethink their clothes again to 'get in the right frame of mind' for a different kind of work space.

In both these examples, we are seeing a very simple but often overlooked fact: wearing the right clothes puts us in the right mental state for the task we are doing. And it all has its foundations in the idea of ritual. Ritual is what makes us humans the way we are. We love it. And so do our children. A key step, therefore, in creating an environment where children can feel happy about sitting down and doing their homework is for them to set aside a favourite T-shirt, top, baseball cap, scarf or any other special item of clothing, and wear it when they work. This item starts to form a part of a ritual that supports homework: when they are wearing it, they focus and get on with their work. Using this technique with children makes them think, 'Once I have my thinking cap on I am working,' or 'Hey, this is my study T-shirt – I am busy now doing my homework.' They have trained their brain that when they are wearing that item of clothing, they are doing their homework.

## STEP 4

### Creating an atmosphere for learning

If you are having people round for dinner, you use music to 'set the scene'. If a company is launching a new product, it uses music to set a tone of expectation. It is exactly the same for homework and learning. In earlier chapters you and your child saw that Baroque music is beneficial to our learning because it works with the brain's own natural rhythms. Baroque CDs cost peanuts at most superstores, and while they may take a bit of getting used to for children, let them experiment with it.

Make sure they understand the science of how brain music works by revisiting pages 64–5. In my workshops, I have never had a child argue with anything that can help them better their study. Communicate the features and benefits and most humans will usually accept an idea where they can see what is in it for them.

The simple fact is that Baroque music, played regularly as background music to homework, can become a positive mental trigger. When the brain hears the music it knows it needs to get ready to study and focus. It's all about creating the right

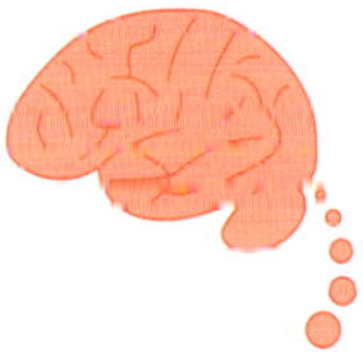

**Brilliant fact!**

The world over, the importance of ritual and habit in the human psyche is borne over time and again. It is therefore important when using these steps that children learn about the cycle of achievement that is set up in their brain once they understand the link between good results and getting into the habit of creating an organized and dedicated work space. In that way, they can start reaping the benefits sooner rather than later.

atmosphere, just like any other event. The right music makes all the difference.

Once you have discussed these features and benefits with your child, next time you are in a superstore, let them choose a couple of Baroque CDs with you and experiment with them at homework time. Played on headphones it can also be a great way for children to block out the noise of siblings and other distractions when trying to focus.

## STEP 5

### Making a special note of ideas

All brilliant thinkers have a special place so that whenever a question or good idea for their work pops into their mind, they can make a note of it. Some children prefer to have different coloured sticky notes that they keep somewhere for reference later. Either way, having a handy and consistent place in which to store and keep ideas is a good habit for children to get into, especially when doing project-type homework that lasts over a term. Whenever they come up with an idea for the project, they can jot it down so that they can refer back to it later.

Having a special notebook gives value to their ideas. They wouldn't lose a gift token you gave them easily because they are in a special wallet. Similarly, they can learn the value of their ideas by keeping them in a special place.

It is no use talking about making learning their own, as we did in Chapter 3, without children having a stash of coloured paper, pens, pencils, string and scissors to put all that into practice with their homework. Learning and creativity go hand in hand, and both come over us in moods. When the mood is upon them, children need to be able to grasp that moment and have everything right there to act immediately. The moment is lost if they have to dash off to the shops, filch around in their sibling's bedroom or hunt around in the kitchen. So alongside their ideas notebook, make sure that your child has a good stock of readily available materials at hand.

Last but not least, keep a good store of simple star stickers, available from most superstores, for when your child sets and achieves short- and long-term goals as discussed on pages 118–27. If children always have a star to hand to reward themselves when they have stuck to their goals and worked to make them happen, they are developing a simple habit that will put them in good stead for a lifetime. Simple but good habits are worth cultivating.

Developing a natural routine for doing homework for children will be helped by them having a special place, but always let them find their own routines for getting things done. As long as it is working, support and nurture it, don't try to change it. If it works for them, that is all that counts in the end. The only time to ever feel the need to have a chat with your child is if the current routine isn't working – and when you do have a chat, emphasize that this is about your child, not you.

Starting from that angle, like most humans, children will respond better to thinking about adapting things a little because they will see the benefit to themselves, as opposed to seeing it as something that they have to do in order to suit someone else's needs. Children are like adults, if they are making changes to suit themselves, they will always want to give it a go.

By following these steps, you will have created the DIY work space your child needs to make learning a rewarding and effective part of both of your lives.

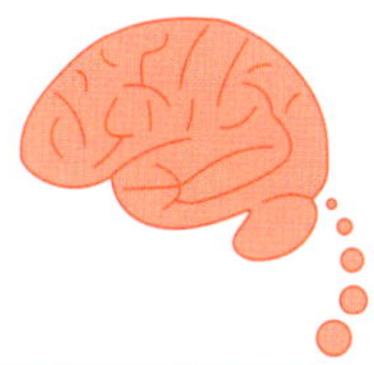

**Brilliant fact!**

When it comes to your child's homework space – think Orange Bowl, think Wembley, think Wimbledon, think 'sacred space'. Treat a child's homework space with utmost respect and then your child will too. The psychological spin-off is that more importantly they will then respect what that space is associated with: their goals and doing the homework and/or short-term goals that go towards achieving them. And that is how great homework habits are born.

# A **word** to the **wise** about **computers**

Whenever a new invention comes out, children's minds are more open to accept them than we are. When books were first invented, people pounced upon them with glee precisely because they could see how brilliant they were. Change happens and with it comes benefits and new challenges. So, before moving on to computers and children, I would like to talk about statistics. Right now, with the advent of DVDs, mobile technology, computer games and burgeoning in-home entertainment, there is real fight on for your wallet in the market place. The fight is between established goods and new ones. It is therefore not unusual for some research and the resultant statistics to be funded by people who can benefit from the findings. This is rife in every industry. Whenever you hear either positive or negative statistics about computer games and children, listen to see who funded the research and was it really independent research?

## EDUTAINMENT WITH COMPUTERS IS GOOD

Computers offer our children the next step in accelerated learning. Remember from pages 62–3 that what children hear, see and touch they remember better, for longer. The interactive, visual and universal capabilities that computers offer children today reinvigorate the concept of learning as an exciting one. Two decades ago I was privileged to be able to learn the grammar of a language that I was studying using a computer-aided system. Having the computer train me meant that I could go back over what I wanted, when I wanted, and move on at my own pace. There are massive advantages to this for the individual and especially for children and this is what the new generation of computer learning – or edutainment – is all about. Edutainment mixes this great capability of learning from computers with exciting interactive visual media and is a huge and growing field.

Edutainment-based computer games are, of course, very different from computer games, the latter being purely for leisure. Having said that, some computer games do offer more cerebral opportunities for children than others. So, if you are looking to buy a computer game for your child, look for the ones that offer some sort of strategy and/or problem solving for children. These games can be beneficial in developing children's logic and reasoning. In other words, in those computer games that aren't just all about shooting down objects and where the aims are more about thinking through problems, there can be benefits for the brain. Where a child is being asked, for example, to design and build a whole city to support an imaginary nation, or set up an emergency contingency to sort out a disaster area or make a place safe for people to live in, then there is lots of thinking involved. These sorts of games may be pleasurable, but they are also helping children learn about something. Games like these fall into what I call the 'plearner' market, and they offer a very good cerebral workout.

## BALANCING THE BRAIN DIET

Whether we have computers or not, children's ability to read and write is as important today as it always was. Whether in electronic form or not, more than ever we all need to be able to read swiftly through copious amounts of information, emails, reports, presentations and so on. Reading is best learnt where it always has been: that great, handy, practical and portable thing called a book. The success of books such as Harry Potter tells us that children like nothing better than a good book to read. So the key thing here is, let them choose their own reading matter. If they like it they will read it and grow from there. It is that simple.

## COMPUTERS AS A LEARNING AND RESEARCH TOOL

Much of the project homework that is set for children today by schools makes use of the research capability of computers. However, despite this now being a usual practice, children don't necessarily automatically know how to get the best out of their computer as a research tool. Often if they are given research-based project homework, they can end up with masses of pages and pictures printed off from the internet. That isn't research and they need to know that now. To help your child get the best out of research on their computer, work together through the checklist, right, which helps children order their work and manage time so they remain focused on the project and get a good result.

# Helping your child get the best out of computers checklist

✓ Think about a beginning, middle and end to your project. What information do you need to get over and in how many days/weeks?

✓ Make a list of five facts you need to find out. Use your computer to find them.

✓ Set yourself a time limit of 20–30 minutes. Once located and printed, tick them off the list.

✓ Make a list of two pictures you may need. Use your computer to find them.

✓ Set yourself a time limit of 10–15 minutes. Once located and printed, tick them off your list.

✓ What extra fact could you find out that might earn you extra marks? Use your computer to find that extra fact.

✓ Set yourself a time limit of 15 minutes. Jot down what you find and then move off the computer.

✓ Now think 'original ideas'! How can you make your project your own and stand out? Could you design and draw the cover, for example?

✓ Write or type notes from the printouts you have and arrange them into your beginning, middle and end. Arrange the facts and pictures to suit your order.

✓ Bind your project together, finish the cover, put your name and date on it and hand in on time.

# The **route** to **success** 8

This generation of children have been born at an exciting time when new technology is changing the way we live and work. But it hasn't come with a manual to help your child get the best out of it. At the end of this chapter your child now understands the importance of managing technology and how to create a work space that is effective for study using simple brain training techniques.

1 **The importance of time management.** When children are young they are unaware of the importance of time, but when it comes to the distractions around them – MP3 players, DVDs and so on – they need to realize just how much time they can actually waste if they are not careful.

Let your child complete the 'My precious time audit' on page 133 to find out just how much time is spent on what. The audit makes time tangible so children can understand the value of managing it effectively.

2 **Help plan a realistic weekly timetable of activity that works for your child.** Never try to impose a schedule on a child about how time is best used. Imagine how you feel at work when someone tries to do this to you. Your heart isn't in it and so you don't want to do the schedule. The most effective schedules are those you chart for yourself.

Visit 'Technology management schedule' on page 133 to help children chart out a balanced schedule that makes best use of their time and resources as well as working in time for their brain to rest and sleep!

3 **Let children become self-reliant when it comes to getting things done.** No one can make things happen for us, we have to do this ourselves. Positive affirmation is a great brain training technique that helps us stick to our resolutions.

Make a copy of 'My precious time contract' on page 134 and let your child read it, fill it in and put on a notice board above their work space.

4 **The human brain loves ritual and habit.** Clothes and objects help our brain associate with, and prepare for, any given task. You would never see a football team playing in business suits; they get their special kit on and their brain is prepared for a game.

Read Steps 2 and 3 and the Brilliant facts! on pages 135–6 to help your child set up a work space bursting with positive visual triggers for the brain, and get into the right mental state for learning by always wearing their special 'study' T-shirt, for example.

5 **Wherever your child studies, make it a place they can call their own.** A regular place to do homework is the key to children developing successful study habits; it helps children associate a particular brain activity with a particular time and space. This doesn't have to be an expensive or even fancy place. Just somewhere they can call their own.

Read the Brilliant fact! on page 137 to find out about the psychology underpinning the importance of a regular place for children to study.

6 **Edutainment and computer games: get the best out of computers.** Edutainment (where the technology of games meets academic learning), is the future for education. The sheer visual and interactive nature of computers makes them irresistible to the human brain, but for children to get the best out of computers for school projects, they need to know how to manage them to use them most effectively.

Use the 'Helping your child get the best out of computers' checklist on page 139 to enable children to benefit best in their study from new technology.

10 **Your child is brilliant**
Journey's end, journey's beginning

# 9 Living and learning
## Making every day count!

8 **Brilliant work space**
Where brain training and focus meet

7 **Goal setting and achieving**
Teaching your child how to succeed

6 **Working with schools**
Cultivating the foundation for your child's future

5 **Getting the best out of schools**
What to look for beyond the 'tourist route'

4 **Cutting tests down to size**
What every parent should know

3 **How your child learns best**
Different ways of learning

2 **Discovering your child's gifts**
Uncovering hidden treasures

1 **Inside your child's brain**
Understanding the technology

# 9

Despite the advent of mass education, some of the best learning happens on the hop; that is, in children's every day experience. No matter how skilled a teacher may be, how interesting a school is, nothing can replace the magic of learning when children are captured by something in the world around them and want to learn about it. At that moment, everything is right there in front of you; you have the opportunity to help them learn about something quickly and efficiently. In the real world, children have the context and the opportunity to see and experience something as it is happening. As part of our evolutionary process, humans often learn on a need-to-know basis. If they can see the immediate relevance of something, they want to know about it straightaway, and children are no different.

*In my local supermarket as I stood queuing I noticed a family in front of me at the checkout. What had caught my attention at first with some amusement was overhearing the little boy asking his dad for an 'advance' on his pocket money. The little boy was articulate and his argument robust: he needed to have the advance so he could buy a few small plastic toys for himself. The toys didn't cost that much, but the dad wasn't keen on handing over the money there and then. He wanted to see first if his son could add up in his head the total cost of the toys.*

*The boy rubbed his head and tried to guess at the answer, but without success. His dad helped him to add up the toys, but he didn't in the end give the son the money to buy them. Instead, he told his son that as soon as he could add up how much the toys cost and how much money he needed to hand to the cashier to pay for them, any future advance would be no problem. The boy was put out, but as they left, his dad set him straight: "Look son, it is no use having any money at all if you don't know what it is worth or if you have to be dependent upon a cashier and their till to figure it out for you."*

*The dad was right; I am betting that next time that family went to the supermarket the boy would be right there figuring out the total cost of any toys he wanted – well ahead of the checkout queue. We live in an age of easy calculation; children regularly think nothing of handing over a bill to a cashier without adding up for themselves the cost of what they are spending.*

# Making everyday **experiences** count

Children are fast learners when they find a benefit in something. Until it hits them with something real and tangible like their pocket money, arithmetic on a white board at school may mean very little to them. Indeed, it may even bore children if they find it hard to get a tangible reason why they should be learning this and that bunch of numbers.

So, change the script. Get them into the habit of learning to add up in their head any extras at the supermarket that they might want to buy and you are on to a sure fire winner. Make it into a challenge.

For example, set a small amount for each child and say that they can spend that on three 'little extras' when they can figure out which random three items of their choice would add up nearest to the amount. Until children experience something like this, they can sometimes have no clue as to how much the things that you buy them actually cost.

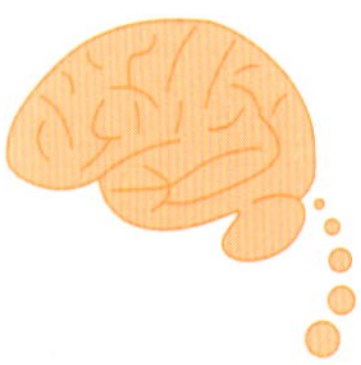

**Brilliant fact!**

In a world where easy credit has made spending a leisure activity, teaching children young the value of your hard-earned cash can only be a good thing for them and you. And nowhere is there a greater opportunity for children to get practical experience of this than by letting them get involved in budget planning for family events and occasions. When they get involved in real life maths situations, they get better at mental arithmetic because what they are doing is no longer an abstract nothing, it is becoming a useful everyday something. And they want to learn more.

## MAXIMIZING NATURAL LEARNING SITUATIONS

Ever heard an eight-year-old try to bargain a better price for their birthday cake at the cake counter? You are about to! Birthday parties are traditionally one of those times when we all like to splash out on our loved ones. And that is great. But all too often it can become a never-ending list of items that, taken bit by bit, seem to cost buttons, but when they start adding up, can become quite a mountain. Getting it right for our children's parties can be stressful too. Are we getting the colour of the plates and napkins right? Is the bouncy castle the one they wanted? Is it available on the day?

May I suggest something? Have a different 'great time' next birthday by letting your child sort out the budget with you. Here is how it works. Ahead of the event set a budget figure that you would normally spend and then, before you spend a penny of it, let your child in on a breakdown of what costs what.

Using 'The thinking child's birthday party', opposite, let your child take a guess at what each of the items may cost that go up to make a birthday party. Make this a fun thing, no pressure, just an open guess at how much things might cost. You may be amazed at the responses. Discuss if there are any areas that your child would like to spend less or more money on. Decide how you are going to allocate the budget, agree it, then set to work buying the items.

# The thinking child's birthday party

Start with the budget for the up-and-coming birthday in front of you. Let your child decide how much they might like to save and/or spend on each of the items needed. Discuss your child's choices and then let your child make the final choices working within the budget.

One of the most immediate things that can come out of this exercise when I have done it with parents and children is that our offspring can surprise us. They can sometimes take the view that rather than have a birthday party they would like to spend the money on something else. I have known children decide to save the money they might spend on buying a cake and ask mum, dad or a sibling to help them bake a cake – another natural maths 'lesson'! Or alternatively they come up with creative ways of making some of the other items themselves. For example, one child decided she could buy a thank-you present for her mum if she saved on pre-printed plates and used a hole punch and coloured ribbon to decorate normal white paper plates.

This needn't be a cost-cutting exercise; that isn't the ultimate purpose at all. Rather, by getting children involved in their early years into a simple real-life situation like this helps them to understand the relationship between money, items and budgets. The big pay-off is that anything they are learning about in maths at school that involves money and budgets then makes more sense to them, because they have actually done it in real life. Plus, of course, if you hadn't already spotted the signs from Chapter 2, if you happen to have a budding 'young tycoon' in your midst (see page 53), this is where they will blossom and decide it is much more fun and practical to use the budget to set up 'Birthday Party Inc.' than spend it on their own birthday party ….

### Use other household practical problem-solving activities

Children love getting involved in anything that involves learning something new. It can be something as simple as helping you prepare for a BBQ with friends, or the next time you are puzzling over some DIY, furniture rethink or garden plans, get your child in on the act. Discuss how many bulbs they think you might need to fill that new window box or desolate patch in the garden? How many packets of seeds could you buy for a certain amount of money? All of this is great for honing their knowledge, getting them thinking and also gaining confidence in problem solving.

Next time your child wants to have friends round for a sleepover, don't do everything for them. Let them get involved putting up the tent, organizing the food and any other arrangements that may need sorting out. By letting them solve practical problems like this, not only are you helping them with real life skills, you are helping develop a greater sense of self-reliance and confidence. At a practical as well as mental level, it really does take all the pressure out of having to think about 'everything'. And the children feel good too. Everyone wins!

## GETTING THE MOST FROM DAYS OUT

Children can learn anywhere, and nowhere is this more true than when you spoil them on a great day out. But no matter how well planned or how much you spent, there is always the question of keeping those curious minds occupied in full. Holiday companies now do a lot to help children get the very best out of their break with you. And days out can be just as much value for money on all fronts, with just a few tips that can make the difference between just another trip and a brilliant trip.

### STEP 1

**Check out what else is going on in your child's schedule**

Before you part with any booking fee or tickets, it is well worth checking with your child that, for example, school isn't going to be going to the same destination in a few weeks' time. There is nothing worse than arriving at the gates of a fantastic attraction, where you paid a fantastic price to get in, only to find the school is taking your child there – next week or, even worse, they have already been! It happens. So, even though you are busy, it saves disappointment all around if you check first.

## STEP 2

**Look at places of interest and activity packs they produce**

Most theme parks as well as museums and historic places of interest, are geared towards school visits. This means that their website will usually feature a whole host of 'What to do and look out for' activity packs for children. These are more often than not downloadable and are well worth printing out before you set off.

I learned the value of doing this the hard way when, having gone somewhere, I found that I had missed something because I didn't read the information beforehand. If you are too busy to do it, remember that self-directed learning means precisely that: get your child to look up the website and download activity packs. If there is a project coming up that may benefit from the visit, your child can make a list of what to look out for. Also, it means that when you get there, you can ask your child to lead the way and show you all the attractions – a great way to help children develop their leadership skills.

## STEP 3

**Avoid the 'Are we there yet?' moment**

As you come up to each motorway exit, pass a landmark, junction or signpost, get your child to find it on a road map and chart your progress as you go. Map reading is a useful skill that is a good way for children to learn orientation, geography, the meaning of distance and the relative time it is likely to take to reach destinations. If you have a satellite navigation system, set your child a challenge to tell you which exit to take before the computer does it for you.

> *Working on a government project, I once took a group of children on a trip to London. When we set off, we were in Manchester, northwest England. After only 30 minutes the coach had to stop to fill up with diesel. As we pulled into the service station, one little boy gathered up his rucksack and more announced than asked: "Is this it? Are we in London?" On the way back from London it was a different story because he understood the distance and the mileage involved.*

## STEP 4

**Enjoy days out for free**

Days out don't always have to be things that end in the 'inevitable' gift shops and involve chequebooks. The *Make your Child Brilliant* journey is about using every opportunity for learning. And that can easily be a family walk in the park on a crisp autumn morning, kicking up the leaves and collecting different ones to take home, find out about and make a collage with.

Before you reach into your wallet think of the other options available. Getting out and about is not about where you go or how much it costs. It is about what you do when you get there and how much this benefited your child that really counts. So here is wishing you lots of fun, fresh air and great natural learning in the process. You and your child are brilliant. All we have done in this book together is find out how to bring that brilliance out and celebrate it, wherever you are!

# The **route** to **success** 9

Having thought about the different activities in this chapter you and your child will have seen that learning doesn't cost a penny and can be something as fun and simple as going out for a walk, kicking about on a cold frosty morning in the gold and brown of autumn's leaves. Learning does not stop or begin at the school gates. In fact, real life opportunities for children to think about and learn from are every bit as valuable in brain development.

1 **Real life maths learning is a great way for children to develop.** Maths is full of abstract ideas that aren't always easy for children to get a grasp of. But put maths to work in real life and that all changes. A simple thing such as helping your child figure out the weekly shopping budget with you can complement their academic study by making maths real.

Visit the Brilliant fact! on page 144 to give you ideas on how you can help your child succeed in maths just by involving them in ordinary everyday activities. Get your child involved and they may save you money.

2 **Let children brainstorm and problem solve with you.** Thinking and problem solving do not always require tailor-made activities to engage the brain. Everyday life is one big problem-solving activity! There is always a birthday party or big family event just around the corner and these are brilliant opportunities for children to use their brain and gain confidence.

'The thinking child's birthday party' on page 145 helps your child problem solve and figure out what is best value for money, how to work within a budget and still have a great time. Enjoy!

3 **Check your child's social diary before booking a day out.** You have just spent x amount of money, you arrive at your destination, only to find your child is going there on a school trip next week. It happens – simply because today's lifestyles are busy and hectic.

Read Step 1 on pages 146–7 and ask your child if they have already been, or are going to visit, the 'surprise' venue you have in mind!

4 **Get the best value for money from days out.** Most venues are just as keen as you that you get the best value for your money, and they are most likely to work with large school visits so are used to dealing with children.

Visit Step 2 on page 147. Most venues now have a website with activity packs on them, so ask your child to download as much information as possible and think about how best to cover all the key features and attractions during the visit.

5 **Avoid 'Are we there yet?'** Children don't have any idea of time and distance. This is easily remedied by turning trips into brain training exercises – ask your child to help plan the journey with you.

Read Step 3 and the case study on page 147. Then let your child get the map out, discuss all routes including the satellite navigation one, if you have this, and set them a brain challenge or two.

# 10 Your child is brilliant
Journey's end, journey's beginning

# 9 Living and learning
Making every day count!

# 8 Brilliant work space
Where brain training and focus meet

# 7 Goal setting and achieving
Teaching your child how to succeed

# 6 Working with schools
Cultivating the foundation for your child's future

# 5 Getting the best out of schools
What to look for beyond the 'tourist route'

# 4 Cutting tests down to size
What every parent should know

# 3 How your child learns best
Different ways of learning

# 2 Discovering your child's gifts
Uncovering hidden treasures

# 1 Inside your child's brain
Understanding the technology

# 10

Congratulations, you've arrived at this journey's end. It is the perfect time for you and your child to celebrate. Not only have you read and completed all the chapters, you are now experts in knowing how to discover and develop your child's full range of gifts and abilities. Turn the page for the final route to success and, yes, you can wave the chequered flag for together you have completed the journey. Imagine a fanfare of trumpets!

In the true spirit of the *Make your Child Brilliant* tradition, it is with great pleasure that I award you both with a well-earned certificate of achievement (see page 153). There's not just one for your child, but one for you too. Fair is fair, you did this together after all.

Every journey's end is, of course, in a way another journey's beginning. The great and wonderful thing about children is that they don't stand still. Remember that the route to success you have mapped out with your child speaks only of this precise stage and time in their lives and as your child grows and develops, new gifts and abilities are always around the corner waiting to be discovered. With each new opportunity and experience, more doors open, inviting your child to think about further goals and dreams that lie ahead – and with that begins a whole new journey all of its own.

The great thing is that your child now has all the brain training and learning techniques they need, so you both know that whatever your child chooses to do, they will always know exactly how to get the best out of their brain and their own natural gifts. And that is the best gift any parent could ever give their child.

Like stars shining brightly in a clear night sky, your child is brilliant, sparkling with ideas, energy and promise. Wherever you are in the world, with that thought in mind, I wish you and your child, health, happiness and the best of everything in life. Value your gifts always, you are unique.

# The route to success: journey's end

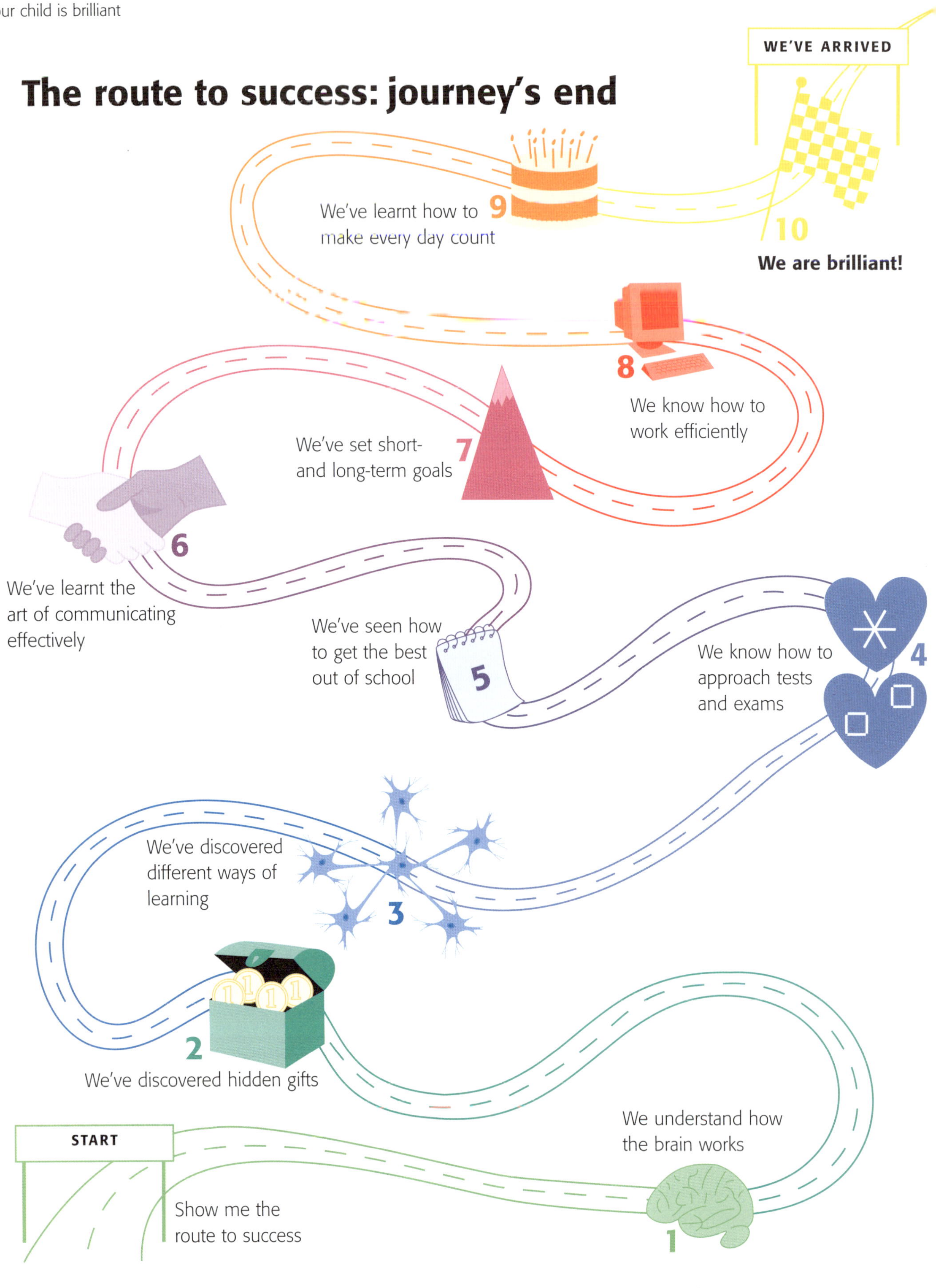

## My brilliant certificate of achievement

I AM
BRILLIANT

Signed ______________________

Date ______________________

## My parent's certificate of achievement

I AM
BRILLIANT

Signed ______________________

Date ______________________

# Further reading

## Autism

Autism is a complex spectrum of conditions in which children with Asperger's also feature. If you want to find out more, the following books give you a wide perspective. Importantly they include extraordinary and personal accounts written by people with austism. These feature first.

*Nobody Nowhere: The Extraordinary Autobiography of an Autistic Girl* and *Somebody Somewhere: Breaking Free from the World of Autism* Donna Williams (Jessica Kingsley Publishers)

*Emergence: Labeled Autistic* Grandin Temple and Margaret M. Scariano (Time Warner International)

*Asperger's Syndrome: A Guide for Parents and Professionals* Tony Attwood (Jessica Kingsley Publishers)

*Understanding and Teaching Children with Autism* Rita Jordan and Stuart Powell (John Wiley & Sons)

## Beautiful Minds

This is a UK registered charity that exists to support research into how to develop the natural gifts in every child. It is important that this research keeps moving forward.
To find out more, visit: www.beautifulminds.co.uk.

## Dyslexia

Spelling has nothing to do with a person's intelligence quotient (IQ). Prior to research, people with dyslexia often had to struggle to demonstrate this against all odds. Top of the reading list below are books that let you gain a first-hand insight from people from different walks of life with dyslexia.

*The Gift of Dyslexia: Why Some of the Smartest People Can't Read and How they Can Learn* Ronald D. Davis and Eldon M. Braun (Souvenir Press)

*Winning is Not Enough: The Autobiography* Jackie Stewart (Headline)

*How to Reach and Teach Children and Teens with Dyslexia: A Parent and Teacher Guide to Helping Students of All Ages Academically, Socially, and Emotionally* Cynthia M. Stowe (Jossey-Bass)

## Neuroscience

Neuroscience tries to understand the brain by thinking about it using a variety of different approaches and perspectives. Globally, the field is expanding rapidly, and much of the text available is academic in nature. The list below should provide an introduction.

*Introduction to Connectionist Modelling of Cognitive Processes* Peter McLeod, Kim Plunkett and Edmund T. Rolls (Oxford University Press)

*The Handbook of Cognitive Neuropsychology* Brenda Rapp (ed.) (Psychology Press)

*Explorations in Cognitive Neuropsychology* Alan Parkin (Psychology Press)

## Testing and ability assessments

Worldwide, testing and assessments to determine children's individual abilities have come into question. The following books provide a thorough insight into the current debates surrounding this issue.

'Assessing Intelligence in a Population that Speaks More than Two Hundred Languages: A Nonverbal Solution' Bruce Bracken and Steve McCallum *Handbook of Multicultural Assessment: Clinical, Psychological and Educational Applications* Lisa A. Suzuki and Joseph G. Ponterotto (Jossey-Bass)

*Cultural Psychology: A Once Future Discipline* M.A. Cole (Harvard University Press)

'You Can't Take It With You: Why Abilities Assessments don't Cross Cultures' Patricia M. Greenfield, *American Psychologist*, Vol. 52 (10) 1115–1124

*Handbook of Multicultural Assessment: Clinical, Psychological and Educational Applications* Lisa A. Suzuki and Joseph G. Ponterotto (Jossey-Bass)

**All references correct at time of publication.**

# Index

# Acknowledgements

If anyone who achieves anything in life is vain enough to think that they did it all on their own, they would be kidding themselves. I would like to extend my thanks to everyone involved in *Make your Child Brilliant*. ★ Robi Dutta and Lisa Opie at channel Five for their vision and support. ★ Sophie and Sam Key and their lovely children, Abigail and Thomas. ★ Benita Matofska and David Pounds at Electric Sky. ★ Vicky Thomas, Dan Roland, Carrie Rose, Alison Vann, Conal Whyte and Amanda Cooton. ★ Emma Pound, for all the perfect cups of Ovaltine that kept me going in all weathers from the Lake and Peak Districts to Brighton beach. ★ Chris and Stewart – the most amazing sound and camera team ever! ★ All the schools and teachers who took part in Manchester, Liverpool, Nottingham, Leeds, London and Brighton – a big thank you. ★ Jane O'Shea and all the excellent team at Quadrille. ★ Luigi Bonomi, LBA Associates, London. ★ My friends Ann and Wayne, Sarah and Darren, Mei Ling and Barry and Saida and Asraf. ★ My long-time advisor Alex Chapman of Campbell and Hooper, London, his partner Georgia and brilliant young son, Macarthur. ★ A particularly helpful staff at Peter Jones, who on a very wet Monday managed to find me a new pair of jeans, wellies and a shirt in under five minutes … ready for filming the next part of a 'parent challenge'. ★ And last but not least, my Dad, Chris, for looking after Tina Tynan who was just a tiny puppy when we began filming and is now a fully grown, big soft, cuddly German Shepherd. Thanks Dad! You're great.

Electric Sky would like to express their thanks to all the children and parents who took part in the TV series *Make your Child Brilliant*, to all the staff of the schools that gave their precious time and patience, to the team at Five and, last but by no means least, to an amazing production team at Electric Sky Productions.

# Answers

**Page 11: a)** False **b)** False **c)** True **d)** True **e)** False **f)** True **g)** True **h)** True **i)** True **j)** True **k)** True

**Page 82: 1)** c **2)** b

**Page 84:** Big, Bun, Deer

**Page 85:** I am very smart, Winner, Brilliant

**Page 86: 1)** d (The pattern is: take the first number, multiply by 2 and then add 1) **2)** e (With the exception of 'e' it is possible to bisect all the shapes equally by drawing a line between the paired triangles) **3)** c (Each design within the different shapes consists of lines. Count the lines and you get a number pattern: 3, 4, 5, 6. 'c' has 7 lines)

**Page 87: 4)** a (The pattern is: Take the first number, multiply by 3 and then add 1) **5)** e (All the other hearts are pointing the opposite way to one another) **6)** b (Each design within the different shapes consists of lines. Count the lines and you get a number pattern: 4, 6, 8, 10. 'b' has 12 lines)